Building Your Home Linux Server

A Comprehensive Guide to Setting Up and Utilizing Your Own Server

Written by, Lynne Kolestar

Table of Contents

Chapter 1: Introduction to Home Linux Servers 4
    History and Benefits of Linux Servers Compared to
    Windows PCs 6
    The Linux Advantage 9
    The Evolution of Windows 12
    Benefits of a Linux Server 13
    Benefits of a Microsoft Home PC 17
    Security: Linux vs. Windows 20
    What is a home Linux server? 22
    Why should you consider setting up a home Linux server?
    25
    Overview of the benefits and uses of a home server 28

Chapter 2: Getting Started with Linux 30
    Hardware Requirements For a Linux Installation 30
        CPU 30
        Hard Drives 31
        LAN (Wired Ethernet) Adapters 33
        Wi-Fi (Wireless) Adapters 35
        Recommendations 36
    Understanding Linux Software and Its Installation 37
        Installation and Initial Setup 38

Chapter 3: Server Administration Basics 45
    Common Server Administration Tasks 45
    Managing users, groups, and permissions 48
    Understanding Permissions 50
    Monitoring system performance and resource usage 56
    Disaster Recovery Procedures 60
    Basic Command-Line Operations for Server Management 65

Chapter 4: Network Setup and Configuration 67
    Types of Networking in Linux 67
    Static vs. Dynamic IP Addresses 70
    DNS (Domain Name System) 70
    Masquerading (Network Address Translation) 71

Chapter 5: Configuring Services 75
    Setting up SSH for Remote Access 75
    Configuring File Sharing Services (Samba, NFS) 78
    Setting up a Web Server (Apache, Nginx) 81
    Installing & Configuring an FTP Server 83

Configuring a Mail Server (Postfix, Dovecot) 85

Chapter 6: Security Best Practices.. 89
Understanding Common Security Threats............................... 89
Implementing Firewall Rules 90
Hardening Your Server Against Attacks 92
Regular Security Audits and Updates.. 95

Chapter 7: Advanced Server Applications..................................... 97
Setting Up a Media Server (Plex, Jellyfin) 97
Minecraft Game Server Installation 102
Setting Up Ham Radio on Linux 108
Exploring Other Advanced Server Applications 109

Chapter 8: Database Integration for Website............................. 111
Introduction to Relational Databases...................................... 111
Designing a Database Schema for a Home Business Website
.... 112
Integrating the Database Backend with a Website 115
Creating and Managing Dynamic Content for the Website 119

Chapter 9: Programming Languages for Server and Website Development.. 121
Accessing and Installing Programming Language Interpreters, Compilers, and Development Environments........ 123

Chapter 10: Future Trends and Further Exploration 125
Emerging Trends in Home Server Technology....................... 125
Exploring Containerization and Virtualization 126

Conclusion 129
Recap of Key Concepts Covered in the Book......................... 129
Encouragement and Tips for Maintaining and Expanding Your Home Server Setup 130

Author's Notes 133

APPENDICES 134
Glossary of Terms.. 134
Resources for Further Learning and Exploration 137

Chapter 1: Introduction to Home Linux Servers

In today's digital age, the concept of a home Linux server has become increasingly relevant and accessible to tech-savvy individuals and enthusiasts alike. But what exactly is a home Linux server, and why should you consider setting one up for yourself? This chapter aims to answer these questions while providing an overview of the benefits and uses of a home server.

A home Linux server is essentially a computer system running a Linux-based operating system—similar to UNIX systems—that serves as a centralized hub for various services and tasks within your home or business network. Unlike typical desktop computers, which are primarily used for personal computing tasks, a Linux server is designed to run continuously, managing and distributing resources to other devices within your network. This can include anything from file storage and media streaming to web hosting and home automation. The stability, security, and open-source flexibility of Linux make it an ideal choice for managing these tasks efficiently and reliably.

The flexibility and power of Linux make it the ideal choice for home servers. Its open-source nature provides unparalleled customization options, enabling you to tailor the server precisely to your needs. Whether you're a seasoned IT professional or simply someone with a passion for technology, setting up a Linux server at home unlocks a world of possibilities. You can create a personal cloud storage solution, host your own websites, or even run a VPN for secure internet access—the potential applications are virtually limitless. Best of all, most of the software available for Linux is free, and you can repurpose almost any PC to run it, making it both cost-effective and accessible.

Moreover, running a home server can be an immensely rewarding learning experience. It offers hands-on exposure to systems administration, networking, programming in various languages, and cybersecurity—all invaluable skills in today's tech-driven world. By managing your own server, you gain a deeper understanding of how the internet and networks operate, empowering you to take control of your digital environment. The sense of accomplishment that comes from successfully configuring and maintaining a Linux server serves as a powerful motivator for many.

In addition to the educational benefits, a home Linux server can also lead to significant cost savings. By consolidating various services onto a single machine, you reduce the need for multiple devices, thereby lowering both energy consumption and hardware costs. Furthermore, the open-source software options available on Linux allow you to access powerful tools and applications without the burden of expensive licenses or subscriptions.

Throughout this book, we will explore the key considerations for setting up a home Linux server, including hardware selection, choosing the right Linux distribution, downloading and installing software, and configuring essential services. By the end, you'll have a solid foundation to begin your journey into the world of home servers, equipped with the knowledge and confidence to build and manage your own.

History and Benefits of Linux Servers Compared to Windows PCs

The evolution of operating systems has profoundly influenced personal and enterprise computing. Among the significant players in this field are Linux and Microsoft Windows, both of which have shaped the way we interact with technology. Understanding their histories and benefits provides valuable insight into why one might prefer a Linux server over a traditional Windows PC, especially in terms of security, flexibility, and performance.

Linux traces its roots back to the early 1990s when Linus Torvalds, a Finnish computer science student, created the Linux kernel as a free and open-source alternative to the UNIX operating system. This initiative was part of a broader movement toward open-source software, which emphasized collaboration, transparency, and community-driven development. Like UNIX, Linux is a multitasking, multiuser operating system, meaning it can handle multiple tasks and users simultaneously.

This design makes Linux particularly well-suited for server environments where managing concurrent processes and users is essential. Over the years, Linux has grown into a powerful and versatile operating system, embraced by individuals, organizations, and enterprises around the world. It now powers a wide range of devices, from smartphones and smart TVs to supercomputers and servers that drive the internet.

In contrast, Microsoft Windows, introduced in the mid-1980s, was designed as a graphical user interface (GUI) for MS-DOS, making computers more accessible to the average user. Over time, Windows evolved into a fully-fledged operating system, dominating the personal computer market with its user-friendly interface and broad software compatibility. Windows PCs became the standard in homes and offices, particularly in environments where ease of use and compatibility with a wide range of commercial software were key priorities.

Despite Windows' dominance in the desktop market, Linux has consistently outperformed Windows in the realm of servers. One of the primary reasons for this is security. Linux is renowned for its robust security features, partly due to its open-source nature. Because the Linux source code is publicly available, a global community of developers constantly scrutinizes and improves it, quickly addressing vulnerabilities and bugs. This stands in stark contrast to Windows, where security patches and updates are controlled by Microsoft, often leaving users waiting for critical fixes. As a result, Linux servers are less susceptible to viruses, malware, and unauthorized access, making them the preferred choice for hosting websites, managing databases, and running critical applications.

Flexibility is another significant advantage of Linux over Windows. Linux offers unparalleled customization options, allowing users to modify and optimize the operating system according to their specific needs. Whether you're running a lightweight server on minimal hardware or managing a large-scale enterprise environment, Linux can be tailored to fit the job. The vast array of distributions (or "distros")—from Ubuntu and CentOS to specialized server-oriented versions like Red Hat Enterprise Linux—means that there's a Linux flavor for every use case. In contrast, Windows is more monolithic, with fewer options for deep customization, particularly at the core system level.

Performance is another area where Linux shines, particularly in server environments. Linux's lightweight architecture allows it to run efficiently on a wide range of hardware, from older machines to high-performance servers. Its UNIX-like multitasking capabilities enable it to manage multiple processes effectively, ensuring stability and reliability, even under heavy workloads. This makes Linux ideal for tasks that require high uptime, such as web hosting, file serving, and database management. While Windows servers have improved over the years, they often require more resources to achieve similar levels of performance, particularly in environments with heavy workloads or limited hardware.

The benefits of Linux servers extend beyond security, flexibility, and performance. The cost is a significant factor as well. Linux is free and open-source, meaning you don't have to pay for licenses or subscriptions to use it. This can result in substantial savings, especially for businesses or individuals who need to deploy multiple servers. Additionally, the open-source ecosystem surrounding Linux provides access to a wealth of free software tools and applications, from web servers like Apache and Nginx to databases like MySQL and

PostgreSQL. In contrast, Windows Server editions often come with a hefty price tag, and many of the tools and applications require separate licenses.

While Windows PCs remain a popular choice for personal computing due to their ease of use and broad software compatibility, Linux servers offer clear advantages in security, flexibility, performance, and cost-effectiveness. These benefits make Linux the operating system of choice for many who seek a reliable, powerful, and customizable server environment, whether for personal use or enterprise-level applications.

The Linux Advantage

When it comes to choosing an operating system for a server, Linux stands out as a formidable option, offering a range of advantages that make it the preferred choice for both individuals and enterprises. The Linux advantage lies in its combination of security, flexibility, performance, and cost-effectiveness, all underpinned by a robust open-source ecosystem.

One of the most significant aspects of the Linux advantage is its security. Linux is renowned for its strong security features, which stem from its open-source nature. With its source code available for public review, vulnerabilities are quickly identified and patched by a global community of developers. This proactive approach to security contrasts sharply with proprietary systems like Microsoft Windows, where users often have to wait for official updates and patches.

Moreover, Linux's modular architecture and strict user permissions make it much harder for hackers to gain unauthorized access. In fact, Linux servers are often less targeted by cybercriminals because they are inherently more secure and resilient to common attacks, such as viruses and malware, that frequently plague Windows systems.

Flexibility is another key component of the Linux advantage. Unlike more rigid, proprietary systems, Linux offers unparalleled customization options. Users have the freedom to modify and optimize nearly every aspect of the operating system to suit their specific needs. This flexibility is reflected in the wide array of Linux distributions available, each tailored to different use cases—from lightweight versions designed for minimal hardware to full-featured enterprise editions. Whether you're running a small home server or managing a large-scale data center, Linux can be adapted to meet your requirements with precision.

Performance is where Linux truly excels. Thanks to its efficient, lightweight architecture, Linux can run smoothly on a wide range of hardware, from older machines to high-performance servers. Its ability to manage system resources effectively ensures that even under heavy workloads, Linux maintains stability and responsiveness. This makes it an ideal choice for environments that require high uptime and reliability, such as web hosting, database management, and cloud computing. Moreover, Linux's UNIX-like multitasking capabilities allow it to handle multiple processes simultaneously, ensuring that your server can manage complex tasks without slowing down.

Cost-effectiveness is another crucial element of the Linux advantage. As an open-source operating system, Linux is free to use, which can result in significant savings, especially for businesses that need to deploy multiple servers. There are no licensing fees, and the vast ecosystem of free and open-source software available for Linux further reduces costs. Whether you need a web server, a database system, or a content management platform, Linux offers a wide range of powerful tools without the need for expensive subscriptions or proprietary software.

The Linux advantage is also evident in its community support. The global Linux community is one of the most active and collaborative in the tech world. Whether you're a seasoned IT professional or a newcomer to server management, you can find a wealth of resources, including documentation, forums, and tutorials, to help you navigate any challenges. This community-driven support system ensures that you're never alone when working with Linux, and you can always find help when you need it.

The Linux advantage is clear. Its security, flexibility, performance, and cost-effectiveness, combined with strong community support, make Linux the ideal choice for those looking to build a powerful, reliable, and customizable server environment. Whether you're running a personal home server or managing a large-scale enterprise infrastructure, Linux provides the tools and capabilities you need to succeed.

The Evolution of Windows

Microsoft Windows made its debut in 1985, aiming to bring a user-friendly interface to personal computing, which was dominated by text-based command-line interfaces at the time. Windows 1.0 introduced a graphical user interface (GUI) layered atop MS-DOS, which marked a significant shift in how users interacted with computers. This innovation helped democratize computing, making it accessible to a broader audience who found the GUI more intuitive and less daunting than the command-line interface.

Over the years, Windows has undergone a remarkable evolution, with each version building on its predecessor to enhance usability, functionality, and security. **Windows 95** was a landmark release, introducing the Start menu, taskbar, and a more refined GUI, which became the foundation for future versions. This release was pivotal in establishing Windows as the standard for personal computing.

Subsequent versions like **Windows XP** brought stability and performance improvements, making it a favorite for both home users and businesses. **Windows 7** continued this trend, offering a balanced mix of features, speed, and reliability, and it remains one of the most beloved versions among users. The introduction of **Windows 10** marked a shift towards a more unified operating system that could run across multiple device types, from desktops to tablets, reflecting the changing landscape of personal and enterprise computing. The latest iteration, **Windows 11**, further refines the user experience with a modernized interface, improved security features, and better support for hybrid work environments.

While Windows has certainly cemented its place as a dominant force in both personal and business environments, especially due to its widespread adoption and support for a vast array of software, it is not without its drawbacks. The closed-source nature of Windows means that users are often at the mercy of Microsoft's update schedules and licensing fees. Moreover, Windows systems have historically been more susceptible to security vulnerabilities, making them prime targets for hackers and malware.

As we gain deeper insight into the realm of home Linux servers, it becomes clear that their adoption offers distinct advantages over traditional Windows PCs. Linux, with its open-source foundation, multi-user and multi-tasking capabilities, superior security, and unparalleled customization options, provides a robust alternative that empowers users to take control of their computing environment. In the subsequent chapters, we will explore these benefits in greater detail, equipping you with the knowledge and tools to embark on your journey into home server setup and management.

Benefits of a Linux Server

Security

Architecture: Linux's Unix-like architecture is a key factor in its security prowess. It emphasizes user permissions and process isolation, which significantly mitigates the risk of system-wide compromises. By enforcing strict separation of user privileges, Linux ensures that a breach in one part of the system does not easily spread to others. For example, the principle of least privilege restricts users and processes to only the resources they need, reducing potential attack vectors and limiting the impact of any security incidents.

Open Source: The open-source nature of Linux is another critical security advantage. This collaborative model allows a global community of developers to continuously review, audit, and improve the codebase. Security vulnerabilities, such as Shellshock and Heartbleed, are quickly identified and patched thanks to the collective efforts of the community. The transparency of open-source development fosters rapid response to potential threats, ensuring that security issues are addressed promptly and effectively.

Less Targeted: Despite Linux's significant presence in server environments and critical infrastructure, its smaller desktop market share makes it a less attractive target for widespread malware attacks. Cybercriminals often focus on more prevalent systems with larger user bases. However, this does not mean Linux servers are immune to threats. Robust security measures tailored to Linux's unique ecosystem are essential to protect these systems from targeted attacks and ensure ongoing security.

Flexibility and Customization

Distributions: One of Linux's standout features is its diverse array of distributions, each tailored to different needs and preferences. Whether you're considering Ubuntu, CentOS, Debian, or another variant, you have the flexibility to choose a distribution that best aligns with your specific requirements. Each distribution comes with unique features, package repositories, and support structures, catering to a wide range of use cases—from lightweight versions designed for minimal hardware to robust enterprise editions with advanced capabilities. Additionally, Linux distributions are easily installed on any home PC or server, making it accessible for users of all levels to set up and customize their systems.

Open-Source Software: The open-source nature of Linux extends beyond the operating system itself to the vast ecosystem of software available for it. Users can modify and optimize both the OS and its applications to meet their particular needs. This flexibility enables organizations to tailor their systems for enhanced performance, efficiency, And functionality. Whether adjusting configurations, developing custom applications, or integrating various tools, Linux's adaptability supports a wide range of customization options.

Cost-Effectiveness

Free Software: One of the most compelling cost benefits of Linux is that most distributions are free to use. Unlike proprietary operating systems that require costly licensing fees, Linux provides a cost-effective solution for both individuals and businesses. This financial advantage is not limited to initial deployment; ongoing updates, support, and a wealth of free applications further contribute to cost savings, making Linux an attractive option for budget-conscious users.

Lower Hardware Requirements: Linux's efficiency also extends to its hardware requirements. The operating system is known for its ability to run smoothly on older or less powerful hardware configurations. This efficiency reduces the need for expensive hardware upgrades and extends the lifespan of existing equipment. By operating effectively on less robust hardware, Linux helps organizations achieve long-term savings and maintain operational continuity without significant investment in new hardware.

Stability and Performance

Uptime: Linux servers are renowned for their exceptional stability and reliability. They are capable of running for extended periods without requiring reboots, which is crucial for mission-critical applications and services. This high level of stability minimizes downtime, ensuring that systems remain operational and available, which is essential for maintaining continuous business operations and delivering uninterrupted services.

Resource Management: Linux excels in managing system resources efficiently. It employs advanced process scheduling algorithms and memory management mechanisms to optimize performance. This effective resource allocation ensures that CPU, memory, and disk space are used efficiently, even under heavy workloads. The result is a system that maintains optimal performance and responsiveness, supporting demanding applications and high-traffic environments.

Benefits of a Microsoft Home PC

User-Friendly Interface

Graphical User Interface (GUI): Microsoft Windows is renowned for its intuitive graphical user interface (GUI). From its inception, Windows has continuously evolved its GUI to enhance user experience. Starting with Windows 1.0, which introduced a basic graphical layer over MS-DOS, the interface has undergone significant refinements. Each version, from Windows 95 to the latest Windows 11, has built upon its predecessors with improvements in usability, aesthetics, and functionality. This ongoing evolution ensures that users of all experience levels can navigate and utilize their PCs with ease, making Windows a preferred choice for personal computing.

Wide Application Support: Windows supports a broad range of applications, making it highly versatile for various uses. This includes web servers, mail servers, DNS servers, database servers, file servers, print servers, ham radio servers, and game servers. Its extensive application ecosystem allows users to configure their PCs for diverse functions, whether for business, personal projects, or entertainment.

Compatibility and Integration

Hardware Compatibility: One of the key strengths of Microsoft Windows is its extensive hardware compatibility. The operating system is designed to support a wide range of devices right out of the box, ensuring users can connect and use various peripherals with minimal hassle. While most hardware works seamlessly, some devices may require additional drivers or configurations to achieve optimal performance. However, Windows often provides tools and updates to facilitate this process, ensuring broad support for both new and older hardware.

Ecosystem Integration: Windows offers seamless integration with the Microsoft ecosystem, enhancing productivity and convenience. OneDrive, Microsoft's cloud storage solution, allows for easy file synchronization across multiple devices, ensuring that your documents and media are always accessible. Windows integrates well with Office 365, Cortana, and Microsoft Teams, creating a unified and efficient experience. This integration supports a cohesive workflow, whether for personal use or within professional settings.

Gaming and Multimedia

Gaming: Windows is the dominant platform for gaming, with over 96% of Steam users running Windows (Steam Hardware & Software Survey, 2024). The operating system supports an extensive library of games, including exclusive titles and new releases. Features like DirectX 12 enhance gaming performance and graphics, delivering high-quality visuals and smooth gameplay. Windows also offers compatibility with a wide range of gaming hardware and services such as Xbox Game Pass for PC, which provides access to a vast catalog of games for subscribers.

Multimedia: Microsoft Windows excels in multimedia capabilities, providing users with advanced features for both media consumption and creation. DirectX, a suite of multimedia APIs, is crucial for high-performance gaming and rich visual experiences. Windows Media Player supports a broad array of audio and video formats, offering robust playback options. Additionally, Windows supports Dolby Atmos for immersive audio experiences and includes built-in video editing tools like the Photos app, allowing users to perform basic editing tasks with ease.

Enterprise Features

Professional Tools: Windows includes several enterprise-grade tools that facilitate efficient management of IT environments. Active Directory enables centralized management of user accounts, devices, and security settings, simplifying network administration and enhancing security. Group Policy offers precise control over user and computer configurations, ensuring that organizational policies are enforced and compliance is maintained. These tools are essential for managing complex IT infrastructures in business settings.

Support and Services: Microsoft provides comprehensive support and services tailored to enterprise needs. Extended support contracts offer critical updates and security patches for legacy systems, ensuring that organizations can maintain stability and security. Dedicated account management provides personalized assistance and strategic guidance, helping businesses optimize their IT infrastructure. These support services are designed to address the complex requirements of enterprises, ensuring reliable operations and continuity.

Security: Linux vs. Windows

Linux Security

Administrative Privileges: Linux enhances security by default through its approach to administrative privileges. Ordinary users operate with limited access rights, while administrative tasks require explicit elevation of privileges through mechanisms like sudo or su. This separation of user and root access helps maintain system integrity and minimizes the risk of unauthorized changes, allowing for a more controlled and secure environment.

Community Vigilance: The open-source nature of Linux fosters a collaborative and vigilant community. This collective effort is instrumental in identifying and addressing vulnerabilities promptly. For instance, the Heartbleed bug in OpenSSL was quickly discovered and patched thanks to the active participation of the open-source community. This community-driven oversight ensures that security issues are addressed rapidly, often before they can be exploited.

Less Frequent Target: Linux's lower frequency of malware attacks can be attributed to its diverse ecosystem and strong security features. With robust user permissions, extensive access controls, and the transparency of open-source development, Linux presents a less attractive target for cybercriminals compared to more widely used systems. Additionally, Linux's modular design and varied distributions contribute to its resilience against widespread malware.

X Windows Security: In the context of graphical user interfaces, X Windows implements several security mechanisms to protect against unauthorized changes. It uses user permissions and session separation to maintain security. Features like the Xauthority file play a critical role by authenticating users and ensuring that only authorized individuals can access the graphical environment, enhancing overall system security.

Windows Security

Windows Security Center: Microsoft addresses the higher frequency of malware targeting Windows through its comprehensive security infrastructure. The Windows Security Center provides real-time protection and regularly updated security measures. Windows Update plays a crucial role in delivering critical patches and updates, fortifying defenses against evolving threats and vulnerabilities.

Integrated Security Tools: Windows includes integrated security tools designed to safeguard the system from a range of threats. Windows Defender offers antivirus and anti-malware protection, while the Windows Firewall controls network traffic to prevent unauthorized access. These built-in tools are complemented by regular updates that ensure users are protected against the latest threats.

Software Authenticity: Windows employs various methods to ensure the authenticity of software. Features like SmartScreen filter and Windows Defender Application Control help prevent the installation and execution of potentially harmful applications. This system of checks and balances enhances security by reducing the risk of malicious software compromising the system.

Both Linux and Windows offer distinct security advantages tailored to their respective user bases. Linux is renowned for its robust security features, including restricted administrative privileges, proactive community vigilance, and inherent resilience against widespread malware. On the other hand, Windows emphasizes user-friendliness and ease of use, integrating a suite of security tools and regular updates to address evolving threats. By understanding these strengths, users can select the platform that best aligns with their needs, thereby enhancing both their computing experience and security posture.

What is a home Linux server?

At its core, a home Linux server is a specialized computer or device that runs a Linux-based operating system to provide a range of services and functionalities within a home network environment. Unlike traditional desktop computers or laptops, which are generally intended for personal use, a home Linux server is configured to serve multiple users and devices across the household.

Centralized Hub: A Linux server functions as a centralized hub, managing and distributing digital resources throughout the home or business network. Beyond serving as a repository for important documents, photos, videos, and other digital assets, it can also function as a firewall and router for your household or business Wi-Fi or LAN network. This added layer of security is particularly valuable given the common security issues associated with Microsoft PCs in both home and work environments. With a Linux server in place, users can access these resources from various devices, including smartphones, tablets, and computers, ensuring seamless integration and accessibility throughout the network.

Media Streaming: One of the key benefits of a home Linux server is its ability to manage media content. It can stream music, videos, and movies to different devices within the home. By installing and configuring media server software, such as Plex or Kodi, users can enjoy their media collection on various devices, including smart TVs and streaming devices, without relying on external services.

Backup Solutions: A home Linux server can be configured to perform regular backups of critical data from various devices within the network, as well as from external websites. This ensures that important files are securely stored and can be easily restored in the event of data loss or hardware failure. Automated backup solutions can be scheduled to run at regular intervals, offering peace of mind and enhanced data security.

Network Services: Beyond file and media management, a home Linux server can handle a variety of network-related tasks. This includes managing internal network services such as DNS (Domain Name System), DHCP (Dynamic Host Configuration Protocol), and VPN (Virtual Private Network) services. By configuring these services, users can enhance network security, manage IP addresses, and securely access their home network from remote locations. Additionally, businesses can fully operate their own websites with a static IP address or Fully Qualified Domain Name (FQDN), while homes can host their own websites even with a dynamic IP address by using dynamic DNS services.

Customization and Flexibility: One of the significant advantages of using Linux for a home server is its open-source nature, which allows for extensive customization and flexibility. Users can choose from a wide range of Linux distributions, each offering different features and optimizations. This means that the server can be tailored to meet specific needs, whether it's running a web server, hosting a personal blog, or supporting advanced home automation systems.

Continuous Operation: Unlike typical desktop computers, which are often powered down when not in use, a home Linux server is designed to operate continuously. This ensures that the services and functionalities it provides are always available to users. The server's ability to run 24/7 makes it a reliable and consistent resource for managing digital content and network services.

Cost-Effective Solution: Running a home Linux server can also be a cost-effective solution. Many Linux distributions and server applications are available for free, reducing the need for expensive software licenses. Additionally, Linux's efficiency allows it to run on older or less powerful hardware, extending the life of existing equipment and minimizing hardware costs.

A home Linux server is a powerful and versatile tool that offers a range of services and functionalities within a home network. Its ability to centralize digital resources, stream media, perform backups, and manage network services, combined with the customization and flexibility of Linux, makes it an invaluable asset for both personal and professional use. With some basic instruction and a curious mindset, anyone can set up and manage a Linux server in a relatively short time.

Why should you consider setting up a home Linux server?

The decision to set up a home Linux server is driven by a variety of factors, each contributing to the overall value and utility it brings to the table.

Some compelling reasons why you should consider embarking on the journey of home server ownership:

Centralized Storage and File Sharing: A home Linux server allows you to consolidate all your digital content — such as photos, videos, documents, and music—into a single, centralized location. This centralized approach simplifies file organization, access, and sharing. You can create shared folders accessible to multiple devices and users within your home network, streamlining collaboration and ensuring that important files are always available when needed.

Media Streaming and Entertainment: Transform your home server into a powerful media hub by storing and streaming your favorite movies, TV shows, and music to various devices throughout your home. With the appropriate software and configuration, you can access your media collection from smart TVs, gaming consoles, smartphones, tablets, and other devices, providing a tailored and convenient entertainment experience for you and your family.

Data Backup and Disaster Recovery: Implementing a home server allows you to set up robust backup and disaster recovery solutions to protect your valuable data and digital assets. Regular backups of your files and system configurations safeguard against hardware failures, software errors, and unexpected events. This proactive approach ensures that you can quickly restore your data and resume normal operations in the event of data loss or corruption.

Network Services and Security: Enhance your home network's security and performance by deploying various network services and security measures on your server. You can configure your server as a firewall, set up a VPN for secure remote access, and implement intrusion detection and antivirus solutions. By integrating these features, your home server acts as a frontline defense against cyber threats and unauthorized access attempts, safeguarding your online activities and maintaining your privacy.

Cost Efficiency: Setting up a home Linux server can be a cost-effective solution compared to subscribing to multiple cloud services or purchasing separate hardware for various tasks. Linux distributions are typically free, and many software tools available for Linux have no associated licensing fees. This financial benefit, combined with the server's multifunctional capabilities, makes it a valuable investment for home users.

Learning and Skill Development: Managing a home Linux server provides an excellent opportunity to learn and develop valuable technical skills. From configuring network services and managing backups to setting up security measures, working with a Linux server offers hands-on experience in systems administration, networking, and cybersecurity.

This practical knowledge can significantly benefit personal growth and professional development in the IT field. Additionally, Linux environments facilitate learning programming languages and techniques, as the server supports a wide range of development tools and languages. This makes it easier to experiment with and master new programming skills in a practical, real-world setting.

Overview of the benefits and uses of a home server

A home Linux server offers a multitude of benefits and uses that can significantly enhance the functionality, efficiency, and security of your home network environment. One of the primary advantages of a home server is its ability to centralize digital resources. By consolidating files, media, and documents onto a single device, you streamline access and organization. This centralization facilitates seamless sharing across multiple devices and users, ensuring that important data is always within reach.

Enhanced security is another key benefit. A home Linux server can serve as a robust security hub, providing features such as firewalls, VPNs, and intrusion detection systems. These tools help protect your network from external threats and unauthorized access, offering a higher level of security compared to standard consumer devices. Regular backups are crucial for safeguarding valuable data, and a home server can be configured to perform automatic, scheduled backups of your files and system configurations. This ensures that your data is securely stored and can be quickly restored in case of hardware failures or accidental loss.

Transforming your home server into a media hub allows you to store and stream your favorite movies, TV shows, and music. With the appropriate software, you can access your media library from various devices throughout your home, including smart TVs, gaming consoles, and mobile devices, creating a personalized entertainment experience.

Additionally, home servers can manage various network services, such as DNS, DHCP, and VPN. These services improve network efficiency and security, manage IP addresses, and enable secure remote access to your home network, enhancing both performance and usability.

Managing a home server also provides a valuable learning experience. It offers hands-on opportunities to develop technical skills in systems administration, networking, and cybersecurity. Furthermore, it serves as a practical environment for experimenting with programming languages and development tools. Home servers can act as central controllers for home automation systems, integrating with smart home devices to manage lighting, heating, security systems, and other automation tasks, thus enhancing convenience and efficiency in your daily life.

Lastly, utilizing a home server can lead to significant cost savings by reducing the need for multiple devices and leveraging open-source software, which typically comes with no licensing fees. This makes it a financially viable option for enhancing your home network's capabilities. A home Linux server provides a versatile platform that can transform how you manage and interact with your digital environment.

Whether you aim to streamline your digital lifestyle, bolster data protection, or explore advanced network configurations and home automation, a home server offers the tools and flexibility to turn these goals into reality.

Chapter 2: Getting Started with Linux

Hardware Requirements For a Linux Installation

Setting up the hardware and network for your home server for Linux is a crucial step in creating a reliable and secure infrastructure for your server environment. In this chapter, we'll cover the essential aspects of configuring your hardware, setting up your network, and securing your home server's physical environment to ensure optimal performance and safety.

CPU

Does my computer have a Pentium(i386) or an AMD(64-bit) CPU?

For Windows
Right-click on the Start menu and select "System."

In the System window, under "Device specifications", you'll see "Processor" which provides details about your CPU.

For macOS

Open About This Mac:

Click the Apple icon in the top-left corner of the screen.
Select "About This Mac."
Go to the "Overview" tab.

Click "System Report" and select "Hardware" from the sidebar.

Here, you will see details about your CPU, including the manufacturer.

When it comes to hardware requirements, any home PC or laptop can be repurposed to serve as a Linux server, but it's important to ensure that your hardware meets the minimum specifications for your chosen server software. For most modern home PCs and laptops, you'll need to select the appropriate architecture for the server software.

Typically, this means choosing the **AMD (64-bit) or Pentium (i386)** architecture to ensure compatibility with your system. Be sure to verify that your hardware can handle the demands of the server software and any additional services you plan to run.

Hard Drives

A reliable hard drive with substantial storage capacity is ideal for a Linux server, as it ensures ample space for the operating system, applications, and data.

When selecting a hard drive, consider the following factors:

Storage Capacity: Ensure that the hard drive has enough space to accommodate your server's needs, including the operating system, applications, and any data you plan to store. For most home servers, a drive with several terabytes of storage is often sufficient, but this can vary based on your specific requirements.

Reliability: Choose a hard drive known for its reliability and durability. Server environments typically require hard drives that can handle continuous operation and high read/write workloads without frequent failures. Look for drives with good reviews and a reputation for longevity.

Performance: Consider the performance characteristics of the hard drive. Solid State Drives (SSDs) are generally faster than traditional Hard Disk Drives (HDDs) and can significantly improve the performance of your server, especially for tasks involving frequent data access. However, HDDs often provide more storage capacity at a lower cost, which may be suitable for less demanding applications.

Redundancy and Backup: Implement redundancy and backup solutions to safeguard against data loss. Consider using RAID (Redundant Array of Independent Disks) configurations to enhance data reliability and fault tolerance. RAID setups, such as RAID 1 (mirroring) or RAID 5 (striping with parity), can protect against drive failures and ensure data integrity.

External Storage Options: If your server's internal hard drive is not sufficient, you can also utilize external storage solutions, such as network-attached storage (NAS) or external hard drives, to expand your storage capacity.

By investing in a reliable hard drive with adequate space and performance capabilities, you can ensure that your Linux server operates efficiently and can handle the demands of your home network.

Your internet connection type & hardware requirements:

When setting up a Linux server, choosing the right network adapters—whether LAN (wired Ethernet) or Wi-Fi (wireless)—is important for ensuring stable and efficient connectivity.

LAN (Wired Ethernet) Adapters

Advantages:

Stability and Reliability: Wired Ethernet connections generally offer more stable and reliable connectivity compared to Wi-Fi. They are less prone to interference and signal loss, which is crucial for a server that needs to maintain consistent network performance.

Speed and Performance: Ethernet connections typically provide faster data transfer rates and lower latency. This is beneficial for tasks that require high bandwidth, such as file transfers, media streaming, and server-to-server communication.

Intranet (Internal LAN Network): If you're setting up an internal LAN network, installing two Ethernet cards in your computer can be highly beneficial. One Ethernet card should handle the incoming internet connection, while the other manages the network traffic between your home intranet stations and the internet. This setup helps to separate and optimize network traffic, thereby enhancing the efficiency and security of your internal network.

Security: Wired connections are generally more secure than wireless connections because they are less susceptible to unauthorized access and eavesdropping. Physical access to the network cable is required to intercept the data.

Consistency: Ethernet connections are not affected by physical obstructions or distance limitations as Wi-Fi is. This ensures consistent network performance.

Considerations

Cable Management: Using Ethernet requires running cables between the server and the network switch or router. Proper cable management is necessary to avoid clutter and maintain a neat setup.

Installation: Most modern Linux distributions automatically detect and configure Ethernet adapters. However, you may need to configure network settings manually in some cases.

Wi-Fi (Wireless) Adapters

Advantages:

Flexibility: Wi-Fi provides greater flexibility in terms of placement since it does not require physical cables. This can be useful in environments where running Ethernet cables is impractical.

Ease of Setup: Wi-Fi adapters are easy to install and configure. Most Linux distributions support a wide range of wireless network adapters and can connect to Wi-Fi networks with minimal configuration.

Interference: Wi-Fi connections are susceptible to interference from other wireless devices, physical obstructions, and distance limitations. This can affect performance and stability, especially in environments with many competing signals.

Speed and Reliability: Wireless connections generally have higher latency and lower throughput compared to wired connections. For a server environment where consistent performance is critical, this may be a drawback.

Security: Wi-Fi networks are more vulnerable to security risks compared to wired connections. Ensuring proper encryption (such as WPA3) and security measures is essential to protect data transmitted over wireless networks.

Recommendations

For a Home Server: If your home server needs to be in a fixed location and performance is critical, using a LAN (wired Ethernet) connection is usually the better choice due to its stability, speed, and security benefits. However, a WIFI connection is easier to initially get your Linux Server onto the internet during installation. You can always change your internet connection after your software install to suit your Linux Server setup.

For Flexibility: If running cables is not feasible and you need flexibility in server placement, a Wi-Fi adapter can be used. However, ensure that you have a strong and reliable Wi-Fi signal to avoid connectivity issues.

LAN adapters are generally preferred for server setups due to their reliability and performance, but Wi-Fi adapters offer flexibility if needed. Choose the option that best fits your server's requirements and your home network environment.

In terms of network setup and configuration, you'll need to establish a stable and secure connection for your home server. This involves configuring your router or network settings to assign a static IP address to your server, which ensures that it maintains a consistent address on your local network. You may also need to set up port forwarding rules on your router to allow external access to specific services hosted on your server, such as web hosting or file sharing.

Securing the physical environment of your home server is also essential. Ensure that your server is placed in a well-ventilated area to prevent overheating, and consider using a surge protector to safeguard against power fluctuations. Additionally, implement physical security measures to prevent unauthorized access to your server hardware.

Linux operating systems have gained widespread recognition for their reliability, flexibility, and open-source nature, making them an ideal choice for powering home servers. This chapter aims to introduce you to the basics of Linux, guide you through selecting the right distribution for your needs, and walk you through the installation and initial setup process.

Understanding Linux Software and Its Installation

At its core, Linux is a Unix-like operating system that offers a high degree of control over system resources and configurations. Its open-source nature means that the source code is freely available, allowing users to modify and distribute their own versions. This flexibility is a key reason why Linux is popular among tech enthusiasts and professionals alike. Linux is also known for its stability and security, making it well-suited for server environments where reliability is crucial.

Choosing the Right Distribution

One of the first steps in setting up a home Linux server is choosing the right distribution (distro). Linux distributions are variations of the operating system that come with different pre-installed software and configurations tailored to various needs.

Popular distributions for home and business servers include:

Ubuntu Server: Known for its user-friendly interface and strong community support, Ubuntu Server is an excellent choice for beginners. It provides regular updates and extensive documentation.

Debian: Renowned for its stability and extensive package repository, Debian is a versatile choice for those who prioritize a reliable and secure server setup.

CentOS: A free, enterprise-class distribution derived from Red Hat Enterprise Linux (RHEL), CentOS is favored for its stability and long-term support. It's ideal for users who need a robust server environment.

Installation and Initial Setup

Once you've selected a distribution, the installation process is the next step. Most distributions provide an installation guide or wizard that simplifies the process.

The general steps typically include:

Download the ISO File - Obtain the installation ISO file for your chosen Linux distribution from its official website. The

ISO file is an image of the Linux operating system you have chosen and is used to create a bootable installation medium. Traditionally, ISO files were used to create bootable CDs or DVDs. However, you can now use tools to create a bootableUSB stick from the ISO file, which is often preferred due to its convenience and speed.

Create the Bootable Media - Use tools like Rufus or balenaEtcher to create a bootable USB drive or DVD with the ISO file. Rufus or balenaEtcher are popular tools used to create bootable USB drives from ISO files and can easily be downloaded for free at the following URL's:

Rufus: https://rufus.ie or
balenaEtcher: https://www.balena.io/etcher/.

Enter BIOS/UEFI Setup: You will need to enter your computer's BIOS or UEFI settings to configure the computer's boot order so that your CD, DVD, or USB drive is set as the primary boot device.

Step 1 - Power On or Restart Your Computer:
If your computer is already on, restart it. If it's off, power it on.

Step 2 – Enter into BIOS or UEFI: Immediately after powering on the computer, you need to press a specific key **during the boot process** (press the key as it is booting) to enter the **BIOS or UEFI** settings. Common keys include **F2, F10, F12, Delete, or Esc**. The exact key combination varies by your computer's manufacturer, and sometimes a splash screen with this information appears briefly during startup. If you miss the opportunity, you may need to restart the computer and try again or refer to your computer's manual.

Step 3 - Navigate to the BIOS or UEFI Boot Options: Once you're in the BIOS/UEFI setup utility, use the arrow keys or the TAB and RETURN keys to navigate through the menu. Look for a section labeled "Boot," "Boot Order," "Boot Priority," or something similar. In UEFI systems, this option may be located under a "Boot" tab or within an "Advanced" settings menu.

Step 4 - Change Boot Order: In the Boot menu, you will see a list of devices such as your hard drive, USB drives, CD/DVD drives, etc. Use the arrow keys or on-screen instructions to change the boot order so that your installation media (USB or DVD) is set as the first boot device. This ensures that the computer will boot from the USB drive or DVD before it tries to boot from the hard drive.

Step 5 - Save and Exit: After adjusting the boot order, navigate to the "Save & Exit" option or press the designated key (often F10 or Esc depending on the BIOS/UEFI) to save your changes and exit the BIOS/UEFI setup. Confirm any prompts to save changes if necessary.

Step 6 - Boot from Installation Media: Your computer will now restart and should boot from the installation media you've prepared. Follow the on-screen instructions to start the installation process of your Linux distribution.

Additional Tips for Step 6 - Boot from Installation Media:

UEFI vs. Legacy Mode: Some modern computers use UEFI instead of traditional BIOS. UEFI has more advanced features, including secure boot. If you encounter issues, check if your installation media is compatible with UEFI or if you need to switch between UEFI and Legacy (CSM) mode.

Boot Menu Key - Some computers offer a one-time boot menu key (often F12 or Esc) that lets you select the boot device directly without entering the BIOS/UEFI setup. This can be useful if you only need to boot from the installation media once.

Once the computer boots from the installation media, follow the onscreen instructions to initiate the installation process.

During the installation process, you will configure several settings including language, keyboard layout, time zone, and hostname. The hostname is the name assigned to your computer within your network. Although you may enter a domain-like format such as domain.com (where domain is the host name and .com is the top-level domain or TLD), this does not need to be a registered domain name; it simply identifies your system on the local network.

Additionally, you will select your network connection type, choosing between Wi-Fi or LAN (wired Ethernet). This configuration ensures that your system is properly connected to your network for further setup and updates.

During the installation process, you'll be prompted to set up a root password. The root account is the administrative account with full access to the system. It's essential to choose a strong and secure password for the root account to protect the system from unauthorized access.

Additionally, you'll have the opportunity to create a regular user account.

This account is used for day-to-day tasks and should not have full administrative privileges like the root account. Each user account should have its own password, which should also be strong and unique.

Regular users can perform most tasks on the system, but they need to use the sudo command to execute administrative commands, providing an extra layer of security.

Next, you will partition the hard drive. For simplicity, you can choose the Guided Partitioning option, which automates the partitioning process. However, be aware that partitioning can be complex depending on your requirements and storage setup.

After partitioning, you will select the type of server you want to install. For internet servers, you might choose packages such as Apache2 for web hosting, Mail Servers for email, FTP servers for file transfers, and DNS services for domain resolution.

For a home server, setting up the X Window System can be beneficial. It provides a graphical user interface (GUI), which can simplify management and interactions, especially for users who prefer a visual interface over command-line tools.

However, if you're setting up a dedicated internet server, avoiding the X Window System is advisable to minimize resource usage and potential vulnerabilities, as a GUI is not typically required for server operations.

Some common X Window System packages include:

Xorg: The X Window System server providing the basic graphical environment.

Xfce or **GNOME**: Lightweight desktop environments that offer user-friendly graphical interfaces.

Xterm or **GNOME Terminal**: Terminal emulators for accessing the command line with a graphical interface.

These packages enhance the usability of your home server by providing a graphical interface, making it easier to manage and interact with your server environment.

Allow the installation process to complete, and remove the installation media once finished.

You can now log in as 'root' to begin the initial administrative setup tasks, which will be covered in detail later in this book.

Linux Support Forums

As you embark on your Linux journey, you may encounter questions or challenges. Fortunately, a wealth of resources is available through Linux support forums and communities. These platforms offer valuable insights, troubleshooting tips, and a space to connect with other Linux users.

Notable Linux support forums include:

Ubuntu Forums: A comprehensive resource for Ubuntu users, offering discussions on installation, configuration, and troubleshooting.

Debian User Forums: Dedicated to Debian users, this forum provides support and discussions on various aspects of the Debian distribution.

LinuxQuestions.org: A broad forum covering multiple Linux distributions and topics, providing a place for users to seek help and share knowledge.

By exploring these resources, you can gain valuable support and guidance as you set up and manage your home Linux server. Understanding Linux and leveraging its powerful features will help you create a reliable and efficient home server environment tailored to your needs.

Chapter 3: Server Administration Basics

Server administration is a fundamental aspect of managing a home server effectively. In this chapter, we'll provide an introduction to server administration tasks, guide you through managing users and permissions, and cover basic command-line operations for server management.

Server administration involves a wide range of tasks aimed at maintaining the health, security, and performance of the server.

Common Server Administration Tasks

Installing and configuring software packages and services

Most software available for Linux is free and can be downloaded either directly through your package manager or from the package manager's website. For Ubuntu and Debian-based systems, you can use apt to install new software packages. In contrast, CentOS and Red Hat-based systems, including CentOS, and Red Hat Enterprise Linux (RHEL), use package managers called yum or dnf (Dandified Yum) for managing software installations.

These package managers allow you to install, update, and remove software packages and services from official repositories or third-party repositories.

Since we require a firewall be set up to do most things with our Linux Server, we will give a full example of downloading and installing a package named: **ufw** (Uncomplicated Firewall).

For Debian & Ubuntu distributions

Update the Package List: Before installing any new software, it's a good practice to update the package list to ensure you get the latest version available from the repositories.

sudo apt update

One of the first software packages you should set up on your Linux server is a firewall to protect it from unauthorized access while allowing access to necessary ports.

Install ufw using the following command:

sudo apt install ufw

Enable ufw - After installation, you need to enable ufw to start using it. By default, ufw is disabled.

Enable ufw:

sudo ufw enable

Check Status - To verify that ufw is active and running, you can check its status:

sudo ufw status

Setting up ufw for firewall connections
In this example, we will configure UFW (Uncomplicated Firewall) for your FTP server.

To Allow FTP traffic through ufw, you need to add a rule to allow traffic on port 21:

sudo ufw allow 21/tcp

If your FTP server is configured to use passive mode, you should also allow the passive ports.

For example, if your FTP server uses ports 10000 to 10100 for passive mode, you can open this range with:

sudo ufw allow 10000:10100/tcp

Allow SSH Connections - To avoid locking yourself out of the system remotely, allow SSH connections before enabling ufw:

sudo ufw allow ssh

Allow Specific Ports: You can allow or deny other ports as needed.

For example, to allow HTTP and HTTPS for your Web Server traffic:

sudo ufw allow http
sudo ufw allow https

Managing users, groups, and permissions

Managing Users and Permissions: User management is an essential aspect of server administration, allowing you to control access to resources and services on the server.

Here are some key concepts related to managing users and permissions:

User Accounts: Create user accounts for individuals who need access to the server. Each user account has a username and password associated with it.

Creating User Accounts on Debian/Ubuntu

Open a Terminal and Create the User:
sudo adduser username

(Replace username with the desired username for the new account.)

You will be prompted to enter and confirm the new user's password.

You may also be asked to provide additional user information such as the full name, room number, work phone, home phone, and other details. You can press Enter to skip optional fields.

Verify User Creation:
cat /etc/passwd | grep username

Creating User Accounts on Red Hat/CentOS

Open a Terminal and Create the User:
sudo useradd username

(Replace username with the desired username for the new account.)

Set the Password:
sudo passwd username

(You will be prompted to enter and confirm the new password.)

Verify User Creation:
cat /etc/passwd | grep username

Groups: Organize users into groups to simplify permissions management. Users within the same group share common permissions. In some cases, you might want to add users to specific groups to manage permissions more effectively.

Adding Users to Groups (Optional)

On Debian/Ubuntu:
sudo usermod -aG groupname username

(Replace groupname with the group you want to add the user to, and username with the user's username.)

On Red Hat/CentOS:
sudo usermod -aG groupname username

Testing the New Account

Switch to the New User:
su – username

Understanding Permissions

In a Linux system, file and directory permissions determine which users or groups can read, write, or execute files and directories. This is vital for controlling access to sensitive data and ensuring that only authorized individuals can modify or execute files.

Permissions are typically represented by a combination of characters or a numeric value, and they include:

Read (r): Allows users to view the contents of a file or directory.

Write (w): Allows users to modify the contents of a file or directory.

Execute (x): Allows users to run a file as a program or script or access a directory.

File and Directory Permissions

Permissions are set for three categories of users:

Owner: The user who owns the file or directory.

Group: Users who are members of the group associated with the file or directory.

Others: All other users on the system.

Permissions are often displayed in a format like -rwxr-xr--, where each character represents specific permissions:

-     Indicates a regular file (directories have a d).
- **rwx** Permissions for the owner (read, write, and execute).
- **r-x** Permissions for the group (read and execute).
- **r--** Permissions for others (read only).

Managing Permissions

Viewing Permissions

Use **ls -l** to view permissions of files and directories:

ls -l /path/to/directory

(The output shows permissions, ownership, and other details for each file and directory.)

Changing Permissions

Use chmod to change permissions. You can specify permissions using symbolic or numeric modes.

To grant read, write, and execute permissions to the owner, and read and execute permissions to the group and others:

chmod 755 /path/to/file

To remove write permission for others:
chmod o-w /path/to/file

Numeric Mode

Each permission is represented by a number:
Read = 4
Write = 2

Execute = 1

These numbers are added together for each user category.

For example, 755 means:

Owner: read (4) + write (2) + execute (1) = 7

Group: read (4) + execute (1) = 5

Others: read (4) + execute (1) = 5

Changing Ownership

Use **chown** to change the owner or group of a file or directory

sudo chown owner:group /path/to/file

For example, to change the owner to bert and the group to www-data:
sudo chown bert:www-data /path/to/file

Applying Permissions to Website Files

When managing a website, ensure that:

Web Server User Access: For web servers (like Apache or Nginx), the web directory runs under a specific user (e.g., www-data). Ensure that this user has the necessary permissions to read and execute files but does not have unnecessary write permissions.

Example to grant username 'bert' access to the www-data group for your web server's directory access

First, you need to add bert to the www-data group. This can be done with the usermod command:

sudo usermod -aG www-data bert

-aG This option appends bert to the group www-data without removing bert from any other groups.

www-data The group you are adding bert to.

bert The user being added to the group.

Verify Group Membership:
groups bert

Change Group Ownership of a file:
sudo chown bert:www-data /path/to/file

(Here we are setting the ownership of the specified file or directory to the user bert and the group www-data.)

Sensitive Files: Restrict permissions on sensitive files (e.g., configuration files) to prevent unauthorized access. Typically, these files should be readable only by the owner.

Directory Permissions: Ensure directories have appropriate permissions to allow the web server to list and access files but avoid overly permissive settings like 777, which allow anyone to write to the directory.

Root, Sudo and Permissions

Typically, only the "root" user or users with administrative privileges (via sudo) can perform actions related to managing users, groups, or permissions on a Linux system. This involves using commands such as useradd to add users, groupadd to add groups, and chmod or chown to change permissions or ownership of files and directories. These commands are powerful tools for controlling access to system resources and ensuring security and integrity within the Linux environment.

If sudo is not installed, you can install it as follows:

Download, Install, and Set Up sudo for Ubuntu or Debian:

sudo apt install sudo

CentOS or RedHat:
sudo yum install sudo

After the installation is complete, you can verify that sudo is installed by checking its version:

sudo -v

By default, on Debian-based systems, members of the sudo group are granted sudo privileges.

To add your user account to the sudo group, use the following command, replacing username with your actual username:

On Ubuntu or Debian:
usermod -aG sudo username

On CentOS or RedHat:
usermod -aG wheel username

Monitoring system performance and resource usage

Monitoring system performance and resource usage on Linux systems is an essential task for maintaining optimal server operation. Whether you are using Debian, Ubuntu, CentOS, or RedHat, Linux provides a wide range of command-line tools and graphical utilities that allow administrators to track and analyze system resources effectively. These tools help in identifying performance bottlenecks, ensuring that the system runs smoothly, and making informed decisions about resource allocation and optimization.

Command-Line Tools for Monitoring

Linux systems offer powerful command-line tools like top, htop, vmstat, iostat, and sar for real-time and historical monitoring of system performance. The top command provides a dynamic view of CPU and memory usage, showing active processes and their resource consumption. htop enhances this experience with a more user-friendly interface, making it easier to navigate and sort through process information. vmstat offers detailed statistics on memory, processes, and I/O activities, giving insights into overall system health. iostat focuses on CPU and disk I/O statistics, helping to identify issues related to storage performance. Finally, sar, part of the sysstat package, collects and reports comprehensive system activity data, allowing for in-depth analysis of performance trends over time.

Graphical Tools for Monitoring

For those who prefer graphical interfaces, Linux provides tools such as System Monitor and Gnome System Monitor. These X Windows-based utilities offer a visual representation of system resource usage, including CPU, memory, disk, and network activity. System Monitor is lightweight and provides essential monitoring features, while Gnome System Monitor is more feature-rich, offering detailed process management and system information. Both tools are particularly useful for users who prefer a visual approach to system monitoring and want to quickly assess system performance without diving into command-line details.

Performing Backups and Disaster Recovery

Performing backups and disaster recovery procedures on Linux systems is crucial for safeguarding data and ensuring business continuity. This process involves creating regular backups of critical files, databases, and system configurations, and implementing measures to recover data in the event of a disaster. Different backup strategies can be employed depending on the specific needs and scale of the system.

File-Level Backup

File-level backups involve copying individual files and directories to a backup location using utilities like cp, rsync, or tar. This method is suitable for small-scale backups where only specific files or directories need to be preserved. However, it may not be the most efficient approach for large datasets, as it can be time-consuming and resource-intensive.

Image-Based Backup

Image-based backups create a complete image of a disk or partition using tools like dd or specialized backup software such as Clonezilla. This method captures the entire filesystem structure, including operating system files and configurations, making it an ideal solution for full-system backups. Image-based backups are particularly useful for disaster recovery, as they allow for the restoration of an entire system to a previous state.

Incremental Backup

Incremental backups involve backing up only the changes made since the last backup, significantly reducing backup time and storage requirements. Tools like rsnapshot and rsync with the --link-dest option facilitate incremental backups, making them efficient for ongoing data protection in environments where data changes frequently. Incremental backups are an effective way to maintain up-to-date backups without the overhead of full backups each time.

Database Backup

For database-driven applications, database-specific backup tools like mysqldump or pg_dump are essential. These tools export database contents to backup files, ensuring data consistency and integrity. Regular database backups are crucial for protecting application data and enabling quick recovery in case of data corruption, hardware failure, or other disruptions.

By leveraging these monitoring and backup strategies, Linux administrators can ensure that their systems remain resilient, secure, and performant, even in the face of potential failures or disruptions.

Disaster Recovery Procedures

Before Disaster Happens – Creating a backup boot disk now

Every Linux server should ideally have a backup boot disk, also known as a recovery disk, to ensure that the system can be restored or repaired in case of a failure, such as a corrupted bootloader, filesystem issues, or other critical errors that prevent the system from booting. A backup boot disk allows administrators to access the system, perform repairs, recover data, and restore the system to a working state.

Why a Backup Boot Disk is Important

System Recovery: A backup boot disk enables you to boot into a minimal environment where you can repair the primary system, restore backups, or troubleshoot issues.

Disaster Recovery: If the main bootloader (e.g., GRUB) or the filesystem becomes corrupted, a backup boot disk allows you to regain access to the system and perform necessary recovery tasks.

Flexibility: Having a backup boot disk ensures that you are prepared for unexpected system failures, reducing downtime and maintaining business continuity.

Creating a Backup Boot Disk on Debian, Ubuntu, RedHat, and CentOS

Creating a backup boot disk involves downloading a bootable

ISO image, burning it to a USB drive, and ensuring that it has the necessary tools for system recovery.

Here's how to do it on Debian, Ubuntu, RedHat, and CentOS:

1. Download the ISO Image

Debian and Ubuntu:
Download the Debian or Ubuntu installation ISO from the official Debian or Ubuntu website.

Choose the "netinst" ISO for a minimal bootable environment.

RedHat/CentOS:

Download the installation ISO for RedHat from the RedHat Customer Portal.

For CentOS, download the ISO from the CentOS website.

Select the minimal ISO for creating a lightweight boot disk.

2. Create a Bootable USB Drive

For Debian, Ubuntu, RedHat, and CentOS:
When creating a bootable USB drive, it's crucial to identify

the correct device path for your USB drive to ensure that the dd command writes the ISO image to the right location. This prevents accidentally overwriting other important disks, such as your system drive.

Here's a detailed explanation of how to identify your USB drive using the lsblk or fdisk -l commands prior to disaster and prior to creating your USB boot disk:

Step 1: Insert the USB Drive
First, insert your USB drive into your computer. Wait a few seconds for the system to recognize it.

Step 2: Identify the USB Drive Using lsblk or fdisk -l

Open a terminal and type: lsblk
Press the Enter key.

Interpret the Output:
The lsblk command lists all block devices (i.e., drives and partitions) attached to your system in a tree-like format.

Sample Output:

NAME	MAJ:MIN	RM	SIZE	RO	TYPE	MOUNTPOINT
Sda	8:0	0	230.5G	0	disk	
|-sda1	8:1	0	512M	0	part	/boot/efi
|-sda2	8:2	0	230G	0	part	/
sdb	8:16	1	14.2G	0	disk	
|-sdb1	8:17	1	14.2G	0	part	/media/user/USB_DRIVE

In this example, **sdb** is the USB drive, with a size of **14.2G**.

Look for your USB drive by identifying its size and name. Typically, USB drives are listed as /dev/sdX (where X is a letter like b, c, etc.), and they will have no or few partitions under them compared to your main system drive.

Use the dd command to write the ISO to the USB drive:

sudo dd if=/path/to/your.iso of=/dev/sdX bs=4M status=progress && sync

Replace /path/to/your.iso with the actual path to the downloaded ISO file.

Replace /dev/sdX with the correct device identifier for your USB drive (e.g., /dev/sdb).

Wait for the process to complete, then safely eject the USB drive.

3. Verify the Boot Disk

After creating the bootable USB drive, it's crucial to verify that it works:

Insert the USB drive into the server.

Reboot the server and enter the BIOS/UEFI settings.

Set the USB drive as the primary boot device and save changes.

Boot from the USB drive and ensure that you can access the recovery environment.

Creating a backup boot disk is a critical step in maintaining the reliability and recoverability of your Linux server. By following the steps outlined above, you can create a bootable USB drive on Debian, RedHat, and CentOS systems, ensuring that you're prepared to handle system failures effectively. Regularly updating the backup boot disk with the latest recovery tools and kernel versions is also recommended to maintain its effectiveness.

Regular Testing: Regularly testing your backup integrity and recovery procedures is crucial to ensure they function as expected in real disaster scenarios. Without regular testing, you may not realize that backups are incomplete or corrupted until it's too late. Additionally, unexpected issues, such as installing incompatible software that alters your boot sequence, can lead to system failures where you need to recover large amounts of data quickly. Regular testing helps you identify and resolve potential issues before they become critical.

Off-Site Backup Storage: Storing backups in off-site locations or cloud storage services provides additional protection against physical disasters such as fire or theft. For instance, if you have a web server with a MySQL database, you can configure a cron job to automatically back up the data to another server or a cloud storage service at regular intervals. This approach ensures that your data remains secure and recoverable even in the event of a local disaster.

Redundant Storage: Implementing redundant storage solutions such as RAID (Redundant Array of Independent Disks) helps prevent data loss due to hardware failures. RAID can be configured in various levels, such as RAID 1 (mirroring) or RAID 5 (striping with parity), to enhance data redundancy and reliability. For example, in RAID 1, data is mirrored across two or more drives, creating an exact copy of your main drive on another disk. This means that if one drive fails, the mirrored copy ensures that no data is lost, and the system can continue to operate using the redundant drive.

System Restoration: In the event of a disaster, restore backed-up data and configurations to a new or repaired system using the appropriate backup restoration tools and procedures. Troubleshooting and resolving system issues.

Basic Command-Line Operations for Server Management

The command line is a powerful tool for server administration, allowing you to perform a wide range of tasks efficiently and programmatically.

For an in-depth guide to Linux system structure and commands, check out my book series, *The Linux Server Mastery Series*, available on Amazon.

Here are some basic command-line operations commonly used for server management:

Obtaining Command Information: Use commands such as man cd, man ls, and man pwd to access command line or program command line information or to navigate detailed information from Linux manual pages (manpages) use man <program name>.

Navigating the File System: Use commands such as cd, ls the file system and view directory contents.

Managing Files and Directories: Use commands such as mkdir, cp, mv, and rm to create, copy, move, and delete files and directories.

Working with Users and Groups: Use commands such as useradd, usermod, groupadd, and chown to manage users and groups on the server.

Viewing System Information: Use commands such as uname, hostname, and to view information about the server's operating system, hostname, and uptime.

Managing Processes: Use commands such as ps, top, and kill to view and manage running processes on the server.

By familiarizing yourself with these basic command-line operations, you can perform routine server management tasks efficiently and confidently. These commands are also used in X Windows so it is a good idea to discover what they do.

Chapter 4: Network Setup and Configuration

Network setup and configuration on Linux involves configuring various aspects to ensure connectivity and functionality. This includes setting up network interfaces, configuring IP addresses, managing routing, and integrating various types of networking. Here's a detailed look at how to manage different networking situations in Linux, including printers, intranet, internet connections, and more.

Types of Networking in Linux

Intranet Networking
Refers to a network confined to a specific organization or local area, with no direct access to external networks such as the internet. It involves connecting computers and resources within the same internal network to facilitate communication and resource sharing. In an intranet setup, a Linux server can serve multiple roles to support network operations.

Network Server
A Linux server might act as a central hub for file sharing, application hosting, and internal communications within the organization.

Firewall

A Linux server can be configured as a firewall to enforce security policies and control traffic between the internal network and external networks, including the internet.

Router

A Linux server can also function as a router, managing the flow of network traffic between different segments of the intranet or between the intranet and external networks.

Static IP Configuration: Useful for devices like servers or network printers that require a fixed IP address. Configure static IP addresses in the network configuration files or through network management tools like nmcli or nmtui.

Dynamic IP Configuration: Typically managed by DHCP servers which automatically assign IP addresses to devices on the network. Suitable for clients or devices that do not need a permanent IP address.

DNS Configuration

Necessary if you are using domain names for internal resources. This helps translate domain names to IP addresses. A local DNS server can be used to resolve internal domain names.

Example: Assigning a static IP to a network printer and configuring DNS for internal services.

Internet Networking

Connecting a Linux system to the internet involves setting up an interface (eth0, wlan, etc..) to communicate with external networks.

Dynamic IP Configuration: Often used when connecting to ISPs that provide IP addresses via DHCP. The dhclient or NetworkManager can be used for automatic configuration.

Static IP Configuration: Required when you need a fixed IP address for services that need to be consistently reachable from the internet.

DNS Configuration

Essential for resolving domain names to IP addresses. Linux systems can use public DNS servers like Google's (8.8.8.8) or Cloudflare's (1.1.1.1) if not using a local DNS server.

Masquerading (NAT)

Used to allow multiple devices on a local network to access the internet using a single public IP address. Configured using iptables or firewalld.

Example: Setting up a gateway server to provide internet access to a local network through NAT.

Printer Networking

Networking printers involves configuring them to be accessible over the network.

Local Network Printing: Set up a printer with a static IP address and configure it on the network. Use tools like CUPS (Common Unix Printing System) to manage network printers.

Network Printer Discovery: Automatically discover network printers using protocols like Bonjour or LPD (Line Printer Daemon).

Example: Configuring a network printer with a static IP and adding it to the system using CUPS.

Static vs. Dynamic IP Addresses

Static IP: Fixed address assigned manually or configured in network settings. Used for servers, network devices, and any system requiring a consistent address.

Dynamic IP: Assigned automatically by a DHCP server. Common for client devices where constant IP addressing is not critical.

Example: Assigning a static IP to a web server versus using DHCP for employee workstations.

DNS (Domain Name System)

Internal DNS: Used in intranets to resolve internal domain names to IP addresses. Often set up using BIND or dnsmasq.

External DNS: Used to resolve external domain names for internet access. Configured with public DNS servers.

Example: Configuring a DNS server to resolve internal service names while using public DNS servers for external name resolution. This setup is essential for managing internal network services and external traffic, such as when hosting multiple websites.

Masquerading (Network Address Translation)

NAT (Network Address Translation): Used to allow multiple devices on a private network to share a single public IP address. Commonly implemented using iptables or firewalld.

Masquerading: A form of NAT where the IP addresses of internal devices are hidden behind a single public IP address.

Example: Configuring NAT on a Linux router to provide internet access to devices on a local network.

Example Configuration Commands for a Static IP Configuration:

For Debian/Ubuntu:
sudo nano /etc/network/interfaces

Add the following text:
iface eth0 inet static
    address 192.168.1.10

netmask 255.255.255.0
gateway 192.168.1.1

For RedHat/CentOS:
sudo nano /etc/sysconfig/network-scripts/ifcfg-eth0

Add the following text:
DEVICE=eth0
BOOTPROTO=static
IPADDR=192.168.1.10
NETMASK=255.255.255.0
GATEWAY=192.168.1.1

Example Configuration Commands for a Dynamic IP Configuration:

For Debian/Ubuntu:
sudo nano /etc/network/interfaces

Add the following text:
iface eth0 inet dhcp

For RedHat/CentOS:
sudo nano /etc/sysconfig/network-scripts/ifcfg-eth0

Add the following text:
BOOTPROTO=dhcp

Masquerading with iptables (firewall):

```
sudo iptables -t nat -A POSTROUTING -o eth0 -j
MASQUERADE
```

Ensure to save the iptables rules:
```
sudo iptables-save | sudo tee /etc/iptables/rules.v4
```

CUPS Printer Networking Setup:
```
sudo apt install cups
sudo systemctl start cups
sudo systemctl enable cups
```

Allow traffic on port 631, which is the port used by CUPS:
```
sudo ufw allow 631/tcp
```

Access the CUPS web interface at http://localhost:631 to configure printers.

Network setup and configuration on Linux involve managing various networking types, including intranet, internet, and printer networking. You can configure static or dynamic IP addresses, use DNS for name resolution, and implement NAT for internet access. By carefully setting up these components, you ensure that your Linux server is properly connected and secure in its networking environment.

Common networking commands:

Ping: The ping command is used to test the reachability of a host on an IP network. By sending ICMP echo request packets to the target host and waiting for ICMP echo reply packets, you can determine whether the server can successfully communicate with other devices.

Traceroute: Traceroute is a diagnostic tool that traces the route packets take from the server to a specified destination. It shows the path packets follow through the network, along with information such as round-trip times (RTT) to each hop, helping to identify potential network issues or bottlenecks.

Netcat: The Netcat utility is a versatile networking utility that can be used for testing network connections by establishing TCP or UDP connections to remote hosts and exchanging data. It can help verify connectivity and test specific network services or ports.

Telnet: Telnet is a command-line tool used for interactive communication with remote hosts over the network. By connecting to specific ports on remote hosts, you can test whether network services are accessible and functioning correctly.

By using these commands and others, you can effectively test network connectivity and troubleshoot any issues to ensure that the server can communicate seamlessly with other devices on the network.

Chapter 5: Configuring Services

Configuring services on your home server is essential for enabling various functionalities and facilitating communication between devices on your network. In this chapter, we'll guide you through setting up SSH for remote access, configuring file sharing services like Samba and NFS, setting up a web server using Apache or Nginx, and configuring a mail server using Postfix and Dovecot.

Setting up SSH for Remote Access

SSH (Secure Shell) is a secure protocol for accessing and managing remote systems over a network. Setting up SSH on your home server allows you to securely connect to and manage the server from any remote location including a Microsoft Windows system using software such as PuTTY.

Here's how to install and set up SSH for remote access:

Ubuntu or Debian: apt install openssh-server

CentOS or RedHat: yum install openssh-server

Configure SSH settings, including authentication methods and access control.

Open the SSH configuration file using a text editor like nano. The default SSH configuration file is located at

/etc/ssh/sshd_config.

You can open it with the following command:

sudo nano /etc/ssh/sshd_config

In the SSH configuration file, you can modify various settings according to your requirements.

Here are some common settings you might want to consider:

PermitRootLogin: Set this option to no to prevent the root user from logging in directly via SSH. Instead, use a regular user account and switch to root using su or sudo after logging in.

PasswordAuthentication: Set this option to no to disable password-based authentication and only allow login with SSH keys. This enhances security by eliminating the risk of brute-force attacks against weak passwords.

AllowUsers: Specify a list of users who are allowed to log in via SSH. This can help restrict SSH access to specific users.

AllowGroups: Specify a list of groups whose members are allowed to log in via SSH. Similar to AllowUsers, this option allows you to control SSH access based on group membership.

Port: Optionally, you can change the default SSH port (22) to a custom port number to enhance security.

Note: Press then CTRL + O keys to write changes to the SSH configuration file. Then press CTRL + X to exit the nano text editor.

Open the SSH port (typically port 22) on your server's firewall. Install a firewall program on your Linux server. A simple firewall is ufw but there is also the older and more complicated iptables program.

We will use ufw for this example:

Ubuntu or Debian: sudo apt install ufw

CentOS or RedHat: sudo yum install ufw

Check the current status of UFW to ensure it's inactive:
sudo ufw status

If UFW is inactive, you can allow SSH traffic by running the following command:
sudo ufw allow ssh

This command opens port 22 for SSH traffic.

Alternatively, you can specify the port number explicitly:
sudo ufw allow 22/tcp

After allowing SSH traffic, you can enable UFW to start at boot:

sudo ufw enable

Generate SSH key pairs for secure authentication.

Use the ssh-keygen command to generate a new SSH key pair. By default, ssh-keygen creates an RSA key pair, but you can specify different types if needed.

Test SSH connectivity from a remote client using PuTTY from a remote computer with Microsoft Windows to ensure proper configuration.

With SSH configured, you can remotely access and manage your home server using terminal-based commands or SSH clients.

Configuring File Sharing Services (Samba, NFS)

File sharing services such as Samba (for Windows-based systems) and NFS (Network File System for Unix-based systems) allow you to share files and directories between different devices on your network.

**Install the Samba or NFS server packages on your server:
For Ubuntu or Debian Systems:**

apt install samba

For CentOS or RedHat Systems:
yum install samba

Configure shared directories and permissions for file access.

After the installation is complete, you may need to configure Samba or NFS according to your requirements. This typically involves setting up shared directories and configuring access permissions.

Set up user authentication and access control. In most cases, the Samba or NFS server service will start automatically after installation. However, if it doesn't, you can start and enable the service to ensure it starts automatically on system boot.

Use the following commands:

sudo systemctl start smb   # Start Samba service (if not already started)
sudo systemctl enable smb   # Enable Samba service to start on boot
sudo systemctl start nfs-server # Start NFS service (if not already started)
sudo systemctl enable nfs-server   # Enable NFS service to start on boot

Test file sharing connectivity from client devices to ensure proper configuration.

If you've set up a Samba server, you can typically connect to it by entering \\<server_ip_address> in the address bar of the file explorer.

You may be prompted to enter credentials (username and

password) if authentication is required.

If you've set up an NFS server, you need to mount the NFS share on the client device.

Use the mount command with the IP address of the server and the shared directory:

sudo mount server_ip_address>:/shared_directory /mnt/nfs

Replace <server_ip_address> with the IP address of your server and /shared_directory with the path to your shared directory. This command mounts the NFS share to the /mnt/nfs directory on the client.

Once connected, navigate to the shared directory on the client device. Attempt to create, modify, or delete files within the shared directory.

Verify that the changes are reflected on both the server and client devices.

To ensure bidirectional access, perform similar actions from the server to access shared directories on the client devices (if applicable). With Samba or NFS configured, you can easily share files and directories between devices on your home network, enabling seamless collaboration and data exchange.

Setting up a Web Server (Apache, Nginx)

A web server allows you to host websites and web applications on your home server, making them accessible to users over the internet. Two popular web server software options are Apache and Nginx.

Here's how to set up a web server using Apache or Nginx:

Ubuntu or Debian Install:
sudo apt install apache2

CentOS or RedHat Install:
sudo yum install apache2

After installation, Apache2 should start automatically.

If not, you can start it manually using the following command:
sudo systemctl start apache2

To ensure that Apache2 starts automatically at boot, you can enable it using:

sudo systemctl enable apache2

Next, you'll need to install PHP and its required modules. You can install PHP along with commonly used modules using:

sudo apt install php libapache2-mod-php php-mysql

By default, Apache2 does not process PHP files. You'll need to configure it to do so.

Open the Apache configuration file for the default site:
sudo nano /etc/apache2/sites-available/000-default.conf

Add the following line inside the <VirtualHost> block:

<FilesMatch \.php$>
    SetHandler application/x-httpd-php
</FilesMatch>

Save the file and exit.

After making changes to the Apache configuration, restart the Apache service to apply the changes:

sudo systemctl restart apache2

Open a web browser and navigate to:
http://localhost/index.html.

You should see the PHP information page, confirming that PHP is installed and configured correctly.

With a web server configured, you can host personal websites, blogs, or web-based applications on your home server, providing a platform for sharing content and ideas with others.

Installing & Configuring an FTP Server

In this example, we will install an FTP server using the package managers available for different Linux distributions. The vsftpd software will facilitate FTP (File Transfer Protocol) connections, which can be used for tasks such as managing files on your website. We will also provide instructions on configuring basic connections through your FTP server.

To download and install vsftpd on Debian or Ubuntu-based systems using apt, follow these steps:

sudo apt update
sudo apt install vsftpd

To obtain and install vsftpd using the yum package manager on CentOS or Red Hat-based systems, follow these steps:

sudo yum install vsftpd

For newer CentOS or Red Hat systems that use dnf:
sudo dnf install vsftpd

Using a simple Linux text editor called 'nano', we will open and edit the configuration file for vsftpd:

(Note: Nano commands can be seen at the bottom of the nano screen. CTRL+C aborts most Linux commands.)

nano /etc/vsftpd.conf

Here's the configuration script rewritten for vsftpd (Very Secure FTP Daemon) with equivalent settings:

```
# Example vsftpd Server Configuration Script

# Set server name (vsftpd does not have a direct "ServerName"
# option, but you can set the hostname or description)

# To display the server name, you can configure the banner
banner_file=/etc/vsftpd/banner.txt

# Configure IP Address and Port
listen=YES                 # Enable listening mode
listen_address=0.0.0.0     # Listens on all available IP addresses
listen_port=21             # Default FTP port
pasv_min_port=50000        # Passive mode minimum port
pasv_max_port=51000        # Passive mode maximum port

# Set SSL/TLS Encryption (Enable SSL/TLS for FTPS)
ssl_enable=YES
ssl_tlsv1_2=YES            # Use TLS 1.2 for secure connections
ssl_certificate=/etc/ssl/certs/your_certificate.pem
ssl_private_key=/etc/ssl/private/your_private_key.pem
rsa_cert_file=/etc/ssl/certs/vsftpd.pem
rsa_private_key_file=/etc/ssl/private/vsftpd_key.pem

# Configure User Accounts (vsftpd uses system users or virtual
# users, not script-based user creation)

# Example: Adding user "john_doe"
user_sub_token=$USER
local_enable=YES
write_enable=YES

# Configure Groups (Optional)
# Group settings are handled by system group files (this is optional)
local_umask=022
chroot_local_user=YES      # Users are confined to their home
directories

# Configure Firewall Rules
# Firewall rules should be set directly on the system's firewall
# Using UFW, you can configure rules like:
```

```
# sudo ufw allow 21/tcp
# sudo ufw allow 50000:51000/tcp

# Configure Connection Limits
max_clients=50          # Maximum concurrent connections
max_per_ip=5            # Maximum connections per IP address
idle_session_timeout=300   # Timeout for idle connections in seconds
max_login_fails=5       # Maximum failed login attempts before locking the user out

# Configure Logging
xferlog_enable=YES      # Enable logging of file transfers
xferlog_file=/var/log/vsftpd.log
log_ftp_protocol=YES    # Log FTP protocol activity
vsftpd_log_file=/var/log/vsftpd.log
log_wtmp=YES            # Log login attempts (wtmp)

# Configure IP Restrictions (Optional)
# Example: Allow connections only from a specific IP range
# Add rules in your firewall for IP restrictions
# Example: sudo ufw allow from 192.168.1.0/24 to any port 21

# Save Configuration (Save the config file manually in /etc/vsftpd.conf)
# Restart Server to Apply Changes (Restart vsftpd after configuration)
# sudo systemctl restart vsftpd

# End of Configuration Script
```

Configuring a Mail Server (Postfix, Dovecot)

Setting up a mail server allows you to send and receive emails from your own domain using your home server. Two popular mail server software options are Postfix (for sending emails) and Dovecot (for receiving and accessing emails).

Here's how to configure a mail server using Postfix and Dovecot:

Ubunto or Debian System Install of Postfix and Dovecot:

sudo apt install postfix dovecot-core dovecot-imapd dovecot-pop3d

CentOS or RedHat Install of Postfix and Dovecot:
sudo yum install postfix dovecot-core dovecot-imapd dovecot-pop3d

Configuration

During the installation process, you'll be prompted to configure Postfix.

Choose "Internet Site" and follow the prompts to set up your mail server.

Dovecot's basic configuration files are typically located in /etc/dovecot/. You can customize them based on your requirements.

Start and Enable Services:

CentOS or RedHat System Install Postfix and Dovecot:
sudo systemctl start postfix
sudo systemctl enable postfix
sudo systemctl start dovecot
sudo systemctl enable dovecot

Set Up SMTP Authentication:

Add the following lines to main.cf:
smtpd_sasl_type = dovecot
smtpd_sasl_path = private/auth
smtpd_sasl_auth_enable = yes
smtpd_sasl_security_options = noanonymous
smtpd_sasl_local_domain = $myhostname
smtpd_recipient_restrictions = permit_sasl_authenticated, permit_mynetworks,reject_unauth_destination
broken_sasl_auth_clients = yes

#TLS/SSL Configuration:

smtpd_tls_cert_file=/etc/ssl/certs/ssl-cert-snakeoil.pem
smtpd_tls_key_file=/etc/ssl/private/ssl-cert-snakeoil.key
smtpd_use_tls=yes
smtpd_tls_session_cache_database = btree:${data_directory}/smtpd_scache
smtp_tls_session_cache_database = btree:${data_directory}/smtp_scache

Reload Postfix Configuration:
sudo systemctl restart postfix

Configure Dovecot for Authentication:
sudo nano /etc/dovecot/conf.d/10-master.conf

Edit the service auth Section and ensure it looks like this:

service auth {
   unix_listener /var/spool/postfix/private/auth {
       mode = 0666   user = postfix   group = postfix

```
    }
}
```

Restart Dovecot:
sudo systemctl restart dovecot

Chapter 6: Security Best Practices

Securing your home server is paramount to protect your data, maintain the integrity of your system, and safeguard against potential threats and attacks. In this chapter, we'll explore security best practices for home servers, including understanding common security threats, implementing firewall rules, hardening your server against attacks, and conducting regular security audits and updates to maintain a secure environment.

Understanding Common Security Threats

Before implementing security measures, it's essential to understand the common security threats that home servers face.

These threats can include:

Unauthorized Access: Hackers or malicious users attempting to gain unauthorized access to your server to steal sensitive information or disrupt operations with malicious software.

Malware and Viruses: Compromise data, or disrupt services.

Denial of Service (DoS) Attacks: Attempts to overwhelm your server with excessive traffic or requests, causing it to become unresponsive or crash.

Data Breaches: Unauthorized access to sensitive data stored on your server, leading to potential data leaks or identity theft.

Brute Force Attacks: Attempts to guess usernames and passwords to gain access to your server's resources.

By understanding these common security threats, you can better prepare and implement appropriate security measures to protect your home server.

Implementing Firewall Rules

Firewalls act as a barrier between your home server and the internet, controlling incoming and outgoing network traffic based on predefined rules. Implementing firewall rules is essential to filter malicious traffic and prevent unauthorized access to your server.

Here's how to set up firewall rules for your home server:

Enable Firewall: Enable the firewall software on your server to start filtering network traffic.

First, ensure that UFW is installed on your Debian server.

You can install it by running the following command:
sudo apt install ufw

After enabling UFW, it will start filtering network traffic

based on its default set of rules.

Some rules are listed below which you can add to suit your server:

# Allow SSH connections
sudo ufw allow OpenSSH

# Allow HTTP and HTTPS traffic for the website (assuming Apache uses ports 80 and 443)
sudo ufw allow 'Apache Full'

# Allow FTP connections (assuming FTP uses port 21)
sudo ufw allow ftp

Allow SMTP and submission for mail server (assuming mail server uses ports 25 and
587)
sudo ufw allow 25

# SMTP
sudo ufw allow 587 # Submission

Allow MySQL/MariaDB connections (assuming MySQL/MariaDB uses port 3306) sudo ufw allow 3306

Once UFW is installed, you can enable it by running the following command:

sudo ufw enable

By implementing firewall rules, you can effectively control network traffic to and from your home server, reducing the risk of unauthorized access and potential security breaches.

Hardening Your Server Against Attacks

Server hardening involves implementing security measures to reduce the attack surface and strengthen the security posture of your server.

Here are some Server hardening best practices to consider:

Keep Software Updated: Regularly update your server's operating system, applications, and software packages to patch security vulnerabilities and mitigate potential risks.

For Ubuntu or Debian:
sudo apt-get update && sudo apt-get upgrade

For CentOS or RedHat:
sudo yum update

Use Strong Authentication: Enforce strong password policies and consider implementing multi-factor authentication to enhance login security.

Enforce Strong Password Policies:

Open the /etc/login.defs file in a text editor (such as nano or vim) using sudo privileges:

sudo nano /etc/login.defs

In this file, you can set various parameters related to password policies, such as minimum password length, password expiration, and password complexity requirements.

For example, you can modify parameters like PASS_MIN_LEN, PASS_MAX_DAYS, PASS_MIN_DAYS, PASS_WARN_AGE, etc., to enforce stronger password policies.

Save the changes and exit the text editor.

Implement Multi-Factor Authentication (MFA):

Install and configure a multi-factor authentication solution such as Google Authenticator or FreeOTP.

For example, on Ubuntu or Debian, you can install Google Authenticator using the following command:

sudo apt install libpam-google-authenticator

Run google-authenticator to generate a QR code or secret key for each user who will use MFA. This command will prompt you to answer several questions to configure MFA options.

Modify the PAM (Pluggable Authentication Modules) configuration to enable MFA.

Edit the /etc/pam.d/sshd file:
sudo nano /etc/pam.d/sshd

Add the following line at the end of the file to enable Google Authenticator MFA:

auth required pam_google_authenticator.so

Save the changes and exit the nano text editor.

Restart the SSH service to apply the changes:
sudo systemctl restart sshd

Configure SSH to Require MFA

Open the SSH server configuration file (/etc/ssh/sshd_config) in a text editor:
sudo nano /etc/ssh/sshd_config

Find the line ChallengeResponseAuthentication and set it to yes:

ChallengeResponseAuthentication yes

Save the changes and exit the nano text editor.

Restart the SSH service to apply the changes:
sudo systemctl restart sshd

By following these steps, you can enforce strong password policies and implement multifactor authentication on your Linux system, thereby enhancing login security. Remember to test these configurations thoroughly to ensure they work as intended before applying them to production environments.

Limit User Privileges: Grant users only the privileges they need to perform their tasks, reducing the risk of privilege escalation attacks.

Disable Unnecessary Services: Disable or remove unnecessary services and protocols to minimize potential security risks and attack vectors.

Encrypt Data: Encrypt sensitive data stored on your server to protect it from unauthorized access and data breaches. By hardening your server against attacks, you can enhance its resilience and mitigate the risk of security incidents and breaches.

Regular Security Audits and Updates

Regular security audits and updates are essential to maintain the security of your home server environment.

Here's how to conduct security audits and updates effectively:

Perform Vulnerability Scans: Use security scanning tools to identify potential vulnerabilities and security weaknesses in your server configuration.

Patch Management: Implement a patch management

process to apply security updates and patches promptly to address known vulnerabilities and mitigate risks.

Review Access Controls: Regularly review user accounts, permissions, and access controls to ensure they align with security policies and best practices.

Stay Informed: Stay informed about emerging security threats and trends by monitoring security news, advisories, and forums. By conducting regular security audits and updates, you can proactively identify and address security issues, reducing the likelihood of security breaches and minimizing their impact on your home server environment.

Chapter 7: Advanced Server Applications

Beyond basic file sharing and web hosting, home servers can be utilized to run a variety of advanced applications that enhance entertainment, productivity, and collaboration. In this chapter, we'll explore setting up a media server using platforms like Plex and Jellyfin, hosting a personal website or blog with WordPress or Ghost, running a game server for popular games like Minecraft and Terraria, exploring other advanced server applications to extend the functionality of your home server, and even integrating Ham radio functionality for communication enthusiasts.

Setting Up a Media Server (Plex, Jellyfin)

A media server allows you to centralize and stream your media library, including movies, TV shows, music, and photos, to various devices within your home network. Two popular media server platforms are Plex and Jellyfin.

Install the Media Server Software: Install the Plex or Jellyfin server software on your home server.

Add Media Libraries: Configure the media server to scan and index your media files stored on the server.

Set Up User Accounts: Create user accounts for individuals who will access the media server and configure access permissions.

Access Media Content: Install Plex or Jellyfin client apps on devices such as smart TVs, streaming boxes, smartphones, and tablets to access and stream media content from the server.

With a media server set up, you can enjoy your favorite movies, TV shows, music, and photos on any device connected to your home network, providing a convenient and seamless entertainment experience.

Install Plex Media Server – Debian and Ubuntu

Add Plex Repository - Import the Plex public key:

curl https://downloads.plex.tv/plex-keys/PlexSign.key | sudo apt-key add –

Add the Plex repository to your sources list:
echo "deb https://downloads.plex.tv/repo/deb public main" | sudo tee /etc/apt/sources.list.d/plex.list

Install Plex
sudo apt update
sudo apt install plexmediaserver

Start and Enable Plex
sudo systemctl start plexmediaserver
sudo systemctl enable plexmediaserver

Access Plex
Open a web browser and go to http://localhost:32400/web to complete the setup.

Install Jellyfin – Debian and Ubuntu

Add Jellyfin Repository - Import the Jellyfin public key:
wget -qO - https://repo.jellyfin.org/keys/jellyfin_team.asc | sudo apt-key add -

Add the Jellyfin repository to your sources list:
echo "deb [arch=amd64] https://repo.jellyfin.org/ubuntu focal main" | sudo tee /etc/apt/sources.list.d/jellyfin.list

Install Jellyfin Server
sudo apt update
sudo apt install jellyfin

Start and Enable Jellyfin
sudo systemctl start jellyfin
sudo systemctl enable jellyfin

Access Jellyfin
Open a web browser and go to http://localhost:8096 to complete the setup.

Install Plex Media Server - CentOS and RedHat

Add Plex Repository
sudo tee /etc/yum.repos.d/plex.repo <<EOF
[plex]
name=Plex Repo

```
baseurl=https://downloads.plex.tv/repo/rpm/
enabled=1
gpgcheck=1
gpgkey=https://downloads.plex.tv/plex-keys/PlexSign.key
EOF
```

Install Plex
```
sudo yum install plexmediaserver
```

Start and Enable Plex
```
sudo systemctl start plexmediaserver
sudo systemctl enable plexmediaserver
```

Access Plex
Open a web browser and go to http://localhost:32400/web to complete the setup.

Jellyfin - CentOS and RedHat

Add Jellyfin Repository
```
sudo tee /etc/yum.repos.d/jellyfin.repo <<EOF
[jellyfin]
name=Jellyfin Repository
baseurl=https://repo.jellyfin.org/centos/8/
enabled=1
gpgcheck=1
gpgkey=https://repo.jellyfin.org/keys/jellyfin_team.asc
EOF
```

Install Jellyfin
```
sudo yum install jellyfin
```

Start and Enable Jellyfin
sudo systemctl start jellyfin
sudo systemctl enable jellyfin

Access Jellyfin
Open a web browser and go to http://localhost:8096 to complete the setup.

Common Steps for All Distributions

Configure Firewall Rules: Ensure the firewall allows traffic on the required ports (Plex uses port 32400 by default, and Jellyfin uses port 8096 by default). Use ufw on Debian/Ubuntu or firewalld on CentOS/RedHat.

Add Media: Once set up, add media libraries through the web interface of Plex or Jellyfin.

Configure Access: Adjust settings for remote access, user management, and media organization as needed.

Minecraft Game Server Installation

Running a game server on your home server allows you to host multiplayer gaming sessions for popular games such as Minecraft and Terraria.

Download and install the game server software for Minecraft or Terraria on your home server.

Configure Server Settings: Customize server settings, including world generation, difficulty level, and player permissions.

Invite Players: Share the server address with friends and invite them to join your multiplayer gaming sessions.

Manage Server Resources: Monitor server performance and resource usage to ensure smooth gameplay for all players.

With a game server set up, you can host multiplayer gaming sessions, collaborate with friends, and build virtual worlds together, fostering creativity and camaraderie.

Here are instructions to download and install the Minecraft Game Server:

Running a Minecraft server on a Linux server involves several steps, including installing the necessary software, configuring the server, and ensuring that your network setup allows for proper communication.

Prerequisites

Linux Server: Ensure you have a Linux server with a stable internet connection. Common distributions used are Ubuntu, Debian, CentOS, or Red Hat.

Java: Minecraft servers require Java. Make sure you have the appropriate version of Java installed.

Network Connection – Dynamic or Static IP?

Public IP Address: For external access to your Minecraft server, you'll need a public IP address. If your server is behind a router like your WIFI, you must configure port forwarding to allow external traffic to reach your server.

A Public IP address assigned to you by your Internet Service Provider (ISP). It allows your server to be accessible from outside your local network.

Port Forwarding: This involves configuring your router to forward traffic from the public IP address on a specific port (25565 for Minecraft) to the private IP address of your server within your local network. This setup is essential for making your server accessible to players outside your home network.

Dynamic IPs and DHCP:

Dynamic IPs: If your server's IP address is assigned dynamically by your router (via DHCP), it may change periodically. To handle this, you can set up a static IP address for your server within your local network to ensure that port forwarding rules always direct traffic to the correct device.

DHCP Reservation: Most home routers support DHCP reservation (or static DHCP), which allows you to bind a specific IP address to your server's MAC address. This ensures that your server always receives the same IP address from the router.

Masquerading: This is used in scenarios where multiple devices share a single public IP address. It allows devices on a local network to access external networks (like the internet) using a single IP address. However, for making your Minecraft server accessible externally, proper port forwarding is the key requirement. Masquerading primarily handles outgoing traffic and may not directly impact how incoming traffic is handled.

Static IP Address: A dedicated IP Address from your ISP that doesn't change. If your server is already using a static IP address assigned by your ISP no further networking setup is required.

Install Java

Minecraft servers typically run on Java. Install the appropriate Java version with:

For Ubuntu/Debian:
sudo apt update sudo apt install openjdk-17-jre

For CentOS/RedHat:

sudo yum install java-17-openjdk
Check Java installation:
java -version

Download the Minecraft Server

Create a Directory: Create a directory to store the Minecraft server files.
mkdir ~/minecraft_server
cd ~/minecraft_server

Download the Server JAR: Download the latest Minecraft server JAR file from the official Minecraft website or use the command line.

wget https://launcher.mojang.com/v1/objects/[version]/server.jar -O minecraft_server.jar

(Replace [version] with the actual version string from the Minecraft download page.)

Start the Minecraft Server

Run the Server: Start the server with the Java command. Adjust the memory allocation if needed.

java -Xmx2G -Xms1G -jar minecraft_server.jar nogui

-Xmx2G allocates 2GB of RAM (adjust based on your server's capacity).

-Xms1G sets the initial RAM allocation to 1GB.
nogui runs the server without the graphical user interface.

Accept the EULA: On first run, the server will generate an eula.txt file. Edit it to accept the EULA.

nano eula.txt

(Change eula=false to eula=true and save the file.)

Restart the Server: Run the start command again after accepting the EULA.

Configure Port Forwarding

Router Configuration: If your server is behind a router, log in to your router's web interface and set up port forwarding for port 25565 (default Minecraft port). This forwards traffic from your public IP to your server.

Firewall Configuration: Allow incoming traffic on port 25565 in your server's firewall.

For UFW (Ubuntu/Debian):
sudo ufw allow 25565/tcp

For firewalld (CentOS/RedHat):
sudo firewall-cmd --add-port=25565/tcp --permanent
sudo firewall-cmd –reload

Managing the Server

Server Commands: Use commands like stop to stop the server, say to broadcast messages, and op to give players administrative privileges.

Automate Startup: Consider setting up a systemd service to manage the Minecraft server automatically on startup.

Create a service file:
sudo nano /etc/systemd/system/minecraft.service

Add the following content:
[Unit]
Description=Minecraft Server
After=network.target

[Service]
User=minecraft
WorkingDirectory=/home/username/minecraft_server
ExecStart=/usr/bin/java -Xmx2G -Xms1G -jar minecraft_server.jar nogui
Restart=on-failure

[Install]
WantedBy=multi-user.target

Replace /home/username/minecraft_server with the path to your server directory and minecraft with your username or the username under which you want to run the server.

Reload systemd and start the service:
sudo systemctl daemon-reload
sudo systemctl start minecraft

sudo systemctl enable Minecraft

Setting Up Ham Radio on Linux

Ham radio, also known as amateur radio, can be integrated with Linux systems for various communication and experimentation purposes.

Hardware Setup

Transceiver: Connect a Ham radio transceiver to your Linux system via serial port for transmitting and receiving radio signals.

USB or Sound Card Interface: Use a sound card interface to connect your transceiver to your Linux system for digital communication modes.

Software Installation: Install Ham radio software packages such as Fldigi, WSJT-X, and Xastir.

Fldigi: Decode and encode digital modes like PSK31, RTTY, and CW.

-X: Communicate using weak-signal modes like JT65 and FT8. WSJT

Xastir: Plot APRS data for real-time tracking and messaging over radio.

Configuration:
Device Setup: Configure your Linux system to recognize and communicate with your Ham radio hardware, including serial ports, USB devices, and audio interfaces.

Software Configuration: Set up your Ham radio software with frequency settings, nodes, and audio configurations.

Operation:
Use your Ham radio software to communicate with other operators, participate in contests, experiment with digital modes, or engage in emergency communication activities.

By following these steps, you can effectively integrate Ham radio with your Linux system, providing a platform for amateur radio operations and experimentation within the Linux environment.

Exploring Other Advanced Server Applications

In addition to media servers, websites, game servers, and Ham radio servers there are countless other advanced server applications you can explore to extend the functionality of your home server.

Some examples include:

Home Automation Systems: Control smart devices and automate tasks within your home using platforms like Home

Assistant or OpenHAB.

Video Surveillance: Set up a video surveillance system to monitor your home using cameras connected to your home server. Software options include ZoneMinder, Shinobi, and MotionEye.

Virtual Private Networks (VPNs): Set up a VPN server on your home server to secure and encrypt internet traffic when accessing the internet from remote locations.

Containerization and Virtualization: Explore containerization platforms like Docker or virtualization technologies like Proxmox to run multiple isolated environments and applications on your home server.

Chapter 8: Database Integration for Website

Integrating a database backend with a website is crucial for storing, managing, and retrieving dynamic content efficiently. In this chapter, we'll explore the fundamentals of relational databases, designing a database schema for a home business website, and integrating the database backend with a website using server-side scripting languages such as PHP, Python, and more. Additionally, we'll discuss creating and managing dynamic content for the website through database integration.

Introduction to Relational Databases

Relational databases are a cornerstone of modern web development, providing a structured and efficient way to organize and manage data. In a relational database, data is stored in tables consisting of rows and columns, and relationships between tables are established using keys. Common relational database management systems (RDBMS) include MySQL or the new and improved MariaDB, PostgreSQL, and SQLite.

Key concepts in relational databases include:

Tables: Collections of related data organized into rows and columns.

Primary Keys: Unique identifiers for each record in a table. References to primary keys in other tables to establish Foreign Keys relationships.

Normalization: Organizing data to minimize redundancy and improve efficiency.

Understanding these concepts is essential for designing an effective database schema for a home business website.

Designing a Database Schema for a Home Business Website

Designing a database schema involves defining the structure of the database, including tables, fields, relationships, and constraints. For a home business website, the database schema should reflect the data requirements of the website, such as user accounts, product listings, orders, and transactions.

Steps for designing a database schema include:

Identify Entities: Determine the entities (e.g., users, products, orders) that need to be represented in the database.

Define Attributes: Identify the attributes (e.g., name, email, price) for each entity and define appropriate data types and constraints.

Establish Relationships: Define relationships between entities using primary and foreign keys to represent one-to-one, one-to-many, or many-to-many relationships.

Normalize the Schema: Apply normalization techniques to eliminate redundancy and ensure data integrity.

By carefully designing the database schema, you can create a foundation for storing and managing data effectively for your home business website.

Here is a simple example database schema for a list of products where the tables can easily be cross-referenced in relation to each other:

Table Name: Products

Columns in Table Products:

product_id (Primary Key): An auto-incrementing unique identifier for each product.
name: The name of the product.
description: A brief description of the product.
price: The price of the product.
category_id (Foreign Key): A reference to the category that the product belongs to.

Table Name: Categories

Columns in table Categories:

category_id (Primary Key): An auto-incrementing unique identifier for each category.
name: The name of the category.

Example of PHP programming code that will retrieve the category name for Product ID 1:

```
$sql = "SELECT Categories.name AS category_name FROM Products INNER JOIN Categories ON Products.category_id = Categories.category_id  WHERE Products.product_id = 1";

$result = $conn->query($sql);


if ($result->num_rows > 0) {    // Output data of each row
   while($row = $result->fetch_assoc()) {
      echo "Category of Product ID 1: " . $row["category_name"];
   }
   } else {
      echo "No category found for Product ID 1";
}
```

Integrating the Database Backend with a Website

Integrating the database backend with a website involves connecting the website's server-side code to the database to perform data operations such as retrieval, insertion, updating, and deletion. This integration is typically accomplished using server-side scripting languages such as PHP, Python, Ruby, or Node.js. In PHP, there are two main extensions for working with databases: MySQLi and PDO.

MySQLi (MySQL Improved) is a dedicated extension for MySQL databases and offers both procedural and object-oriented interfaces, providing a straightforward way to connect to a MySQL database and execute queries.

However, MySQLi is limited to MySQL databases only. PDO (PHP Data Objects), on the other hand, is a database access layer that supports multiple database types, including MySQL, PostgreSQL, SQLite, and others, making it more versatile for projects that might require switching databases. PDO exclusively uses an object-oriented approach and offers a range of features such as prepared statements and transactions, enhancing security and performance.

While MySQLi might be simpler to use for strictly MySQL-based projects, PDO's flexibility and advanced features make it a more powerful option for complex applications requiring database abstraction and portability.

Steps for integrating the database backend with a website include:

Establish Database Connection: Create a connection to the database server using appropriate credentials.

For Simplicity across different database types we will use PHP PDO to connect to a database:

Go to the HTML directory:
cd /var/www/html/

Create a text file named pdo_queries.php:
nano pdo_queries.php

Enter the following:

```
<?php

include 'db_config.php';

try {
   // Retrieve data
   $sql = "SELECT id, name, email FROM users";
   $stmt = $conn->query($sql);

   $userProfiles = [];
   while ($row = $stmt->fetch(PDO::FETCH_ASSOC)) {
      $userProfiles[] = $row;

   }

   // Insert data
   $sql = "INSERT INTO users (name, email) VALUES ('John Doe', 'john@example.com')";
```

```php
    $conn->exec($sql);

    echo "New record created successfully.<br>";

    // Update data
    $sql = "UPDATE users SET email = 'john.doe@example.com' WHERE name = 'John Doe'";

    $stmt = $conn->prepare($sql);
    $stmt->execute();
    echo "Record updated successfully.<br>";

    // Delete data
    $sql = "DELETE FROM users WHERE name = 'John Doe'";
    $stmt = $conn->prepare($sql);
    $stmt->execute();
    echo "Record deleted successfully.<br>";

} catch(PDOException $e) {
    echo "Error: " . $e->getMessage();
}

// Close connection
$conn = null;

?>

<!DOCTYPE html>
<html>
<head>
   <title>User Profiles</title>
</head>
<body>
   <h1>User Profiles</h1>
   <table border="1">
     <tr>
       <th>ID</th>
```

```
      <th>Name</th>
      <th>Email</th>
    </tr>
    <?php if (!empty($userProfiles)): ?>
      <?php foreach ($userProfiles as $profile): ?>
        <tr>
          <td><?php echo htmlspecialchars($profile['id']); ?></td>
          <td><?php echo htmlspecialchars($profile['name']); ?></td>
          <td><?php echo htmlspecialchars($profile['email']); ?></td>
        </tr>
      <?php endforeach; ?>
    <?php else: ?>
      <tr>
        <td colspan="3">No user profiles found.</td>
      </tr>
    <?php endif; ?>
  </table>
</body>
</html>
```

Note: Press CTRL+O to Save the file. Press CTRL+Z to exit the nano text editor.

By integrating the database backend with the website, you can create a dynamic and interactive user experience that responds to user input and updates in real-time.

Creating and Managing Dynamic Content for the Website

With the database backend integrated into the website, you can create and manage dynamic content efficiently. Dynamic content allows for personalized user experiences, real-time updates, and interactive features. Common examples of dynamic content for a home business website include user profiles, product catalogs, shopping carts, and order tracking.

Key considerations for creating and managing dynamic content include:

Data Validation: Validate user input to ensure data integrity and prevent security vulnerabilities such as SQL injection.

Session Management: Manage user sessions to maintain stateful interactions and track user activity across multiple pages.

Caching: Implement caching mechanisms to improve performance and reduce database load by storing frequently accessed data in memory or disk.

Scalability: Design the website and database architecture to scale horizontally or vertically to accommodate growth in traffic and data volume.

By leveraging the power of database integration, you can create a dynamic and engaging website that meets the needs of your home business and provides value to your customers.

Chapter 9: Programming Languages for Server and Website Development

Programming languages play a crucial role in server-side and website development, providing the tools and frameworks necessary to build dynamic and interactive web applications. In this chapter, we'll provide an overview of programming languages commonly used for server-side and website development, discuss the ease of creating programs for servers and websites in various languages, and explore accessing and installing programming language interpreters, compilers, and development environments.

In web development, server-side languages handle operations on the server, like processing user requests and accessing databases, while client-side languages manage interactions within the user's browser, such as rendering user interfaces and executing scripts.

Overview of Programming Languages

A wide variety of programming languages are used for server-side and website development, each offering different features, syntax, and frameworks tailored to specific use cases and preferences.

Each programming language has its strengths and weaknesses, and the choice of language often depends on factors such as project requirements, performance considerations, and developer familiarity.

Ease of Creating Programs for Servers and Websites The ease of creating programs for servers and websites varies depending on the programming language and the developer's experience and proficiency.

Some factors that contribute to the ease of development include:

Syntax and Readability: Languages with clear and concise syntax, such as Python and Ruby, are often considered easier to learn and use.

Frameworks and Libraries: Frameworks and libraries provide pre-built components and abstractions that streamline development and simplify common tasks.

Community and Documentation: Strong community support and comprehensive documentation make it easier to find resources, tutorials, and solutions to problems.

Tooling and IDE Support: Integrated development environments (IDEs) and developer tools with features like code completion, debugging, and refactoring can improve productivity and ease of development.

Ultimately, the ease of creating programs for servers and websites depends on the developer's familiarity with the language, the available tools and resources, and the complexity of the project.

Accessing and Installing Programming Language Interpreters, Compilers, and Development Environments

Accessing and installing programming language interpreters, compilers, and development environments is straightforward and varies depending on the programming language and platform. Most programming languages provide official websites or repositories where you can download the necessary tools and documentation. If you have followed this book, we have installed the PHP Language.

Steps for accessing and installing programming language tools and environments include:

Download the Interpreter or Compiler: Visit the official website or repository for the programming language and download the appropriate interpreter or compiler for your operating system.

Install the Development Environment:
Optionally, install a development environment or IDE tailored to the programming language, such as Visual Studio Code for JavaScript or PyCharm for Python.

Set Up Environment Variables: Configure environment variables and system paths as needed to ensure that the interpreter or compiler is accessible from the command line.

Install Dependencies and Packages: Depending on the

programming language and project requirements, install any necessary dependencies or packages using package managers like npm for JavaScript or pip for Python.

By following these steps, you can quickly set up the necessary tools and environments for developing server-side and website applications in your preferred programming language.

Chapter 10: Future Trends and Further Exploration

As technology continues to evolve, new trends and advancements in home server technology emerge, offering greater capabilities, efficiency, and opportunities for homebased setups. In this chapter, we'll explore emerging trends in home server technology, delve into the concepts of containerization and virtualization, and provide resources for further learning and exploration.

Emerging Trends in Home Server Technology

The landscape of home server technology is rapidly changing, driven by innovations that enhance performance, security, and usability.

Some of the emerging trends in home server technology include:

Edge Computing: As more devices become connected through the Internet of Things (IoT), edge computing brings processing power closer to the data source, reducing latency and improving response times for real-time applications.

5G Connectivity: The rollout of 5G networks promises faster and more reliable internet connectivity, enabling more robust remote access and better performance for home servers.

Green Computing: With an increased focus on energy efficiency and sustainability, new hardware and software solutions are being developed to reduce the environmental impact of home servers.

AI and Machine Learning: Integrating AI and machine learning capabilities into home servers allows for advanced automation, predictive maintenance, and smarter home automation systems.

Enhanced Security: Innovations in security technologies, such as zero-trust architectures and advanced encryption methods, are making home servers more secure against evolving cyber threats.

By staying informed about these trends, home server enthusiasts can leverage the latest technologies to enhance their server setups and achieve better performance, efficiency, and security.

Exploring Containerization and Virtualization

Containerization and virtualization are powerful techniques that enable more efficient and flexible management of server resources. Both technologies allow multiple isolated environments to run on a single physical server, each with its own configuration and dependencies.

Containerization: Containerization involves encapsulating an application and its dependencies into a lightweight, portable container. Containers share the host operating system's kernel but run as isolated processes. Popular containerization platforms include Docker and Kubernetes.

Docker: Docker is a widely used platform for developing, shipping, and running applications in containers. It simplifies deployment and ensures consistency across different environments.

Kubernetes: Kubernetes is an orchestration platform for managing containerized applications at scale. It automates the deployment, scaling, and management of containers, making it ideal for complex and distributed applications.

Virtualization: Virtualization involves creating multiple virtual machines (VMs) on a single physical server, each running its own operating system. This allows for the isolation of different workloads and better utilization of hardware resources. Popular virtualization platforms include VMware, VirtualBox, and Proxmox.

VMware: VMware offers enterprise-grade virtualization solutions with advanced features for resource management, high availability, and disaster recovery.

VirtualBox: Oracle's VirtualBox is a free and open-source virtualization platform that supports a wide range of guest operating systems and is suitable for both desktop and server environments.

Proxmox: Proxmox Virtual Environment is an open-source virtualization management platform that integrates KVM (Kernel-based Virtual Machine) and LXC (Linux Containers) for comprehensive virtual environment management.

By exploring containerization and virtualization, home server users can achieve greater flexibility, scalability, and efficiency in managing their server environments.

Conclusion

Recap of Key Concepts Covered in the Book

In this book, we've covered the essential steps for building and managing your own Linux-based home server. We began with an introduction to home Linux servers, emphasizing the advantages of using Linux over Windows for server management, such as stability, security, and flexibility. We discussed why setting up a home server is beneficial, including cost savings, increased control over your data, and the ability to customize your system to meet your needs.

We then explored the initial setup of your server, from selecting the appropriate hardware to installing Linux. Understanding the right CPU, hard drives, and network adapters for your setup was key to building a system that performs efficiently. After installation, we focused on server administration basics, including user management, system monitoring, and disaster recovery techniques. Basic command-line operations were also introduced, which are essential for interacting with and maintaining your server.

The book also delved into configuring various services on your server to unlock its full potential. From setting up SSH for remote access to configuring file sharing services like Samba and NFS, and hosting a web server using Apache or Nginx, we covered the practical applications that turn your server into a multifunctional tool. We also examined security best practices, such as configuring firewalls, hardening your server, and performing regular security audits to protect against potential threats.

In the latter chapters, we explored advanced server applications like setting up a media server or a Minecraft game server, demonstrating the versatility of a Linux server. Additionally, we discussed integrating databases with websites, programming languages for server-side development, and future trends in home server technology, including containerization and virtualization. By the end of the book, you should be equipped with the knowledge to create a secure, efficient, and adaptable home server tailored to your personal and professional needs.

Encouragement and Tips for Maintaining and Expanding Your Home Server Setup

Maintaining a home server is an ongoing process that involves regular updates, proactive monitoring, and occasional troubleshooting to ensure optimal performance and security.

For a deeper dive into Linux servers, their structure, and command usage, check out my comprehensive book series, *The Linux Server Mastery Series*, available on Amazon. These books provide in-depth guidance to help you explore a wide range of Linux server configurations and enhance your server management skills.

Here are some tips and encouragement to help you maintain and expand your home server setup:

Stay Updated: Regularly update your server's software and operating system to protect against security vulnerabilities and benefit from the latest features and improvements.

Regular Backups: Implement a robust backup strategy to ensure that your data is safe and can be quickly restored in case of hardware failure, accidental deletion, or other disasters.

Monitor Performance: Use monitoring tools to keep an eye on your server's performance and resource usage. Address any issues promptly to maintain optimal performance and prevent downtime.

Learn and Experiment: Continuously expand your knowledge by exploring new technologies, tools, and best practices. Don't be afraid to experiment with new services and configurations to enhance your server's capabilities.

Engage with the Community: Join online forums, communities, and user groups to share experiences, ask questions, and learn from other home server enthusiasts. Engaging with the community can provide valuable insights and support.

Document Your Setup: Keep detailed documentation of your server's configuration, installed services, and any custom scripts or settings. This documentation will be invaluable for troubleshooting and future upgrades.

Automate Where Possible: Use automation tools and scripts to streamline repetitive tasks, such as updates, backups, and monitoring. Automation reduces the risk of human error and saves time.

Prioritize Security: Always prioritize security by implementing strong passwords, enabling two-factor authentication, and regularly reviewing your server's security settings. Stay informed about the latest security threats and best practices.

Building and maintaining a home Linux server is a journey that offers continuous learning and growth. By applying the knowledge and skills gained from this book, you can create a powerful and versatile server environment that meets your needs and adapts to future challenges.

Enjoy the process, stay curious, and keep exploring the exciting world of home server technology.

Author's Notes

This book will guide you through the process of transforming an older home PC into a powerful Linux server. Drawing on years of hands-on experience in setting up and maintaining home Linux servers, I've explored a wide variety of internet server applications and configurations. One key takeaway from my experience is that the process is actually quite simple.

Turning your home PC into a Linux server is both an enriching learning experience and a practical endeavor when approached with clear, step-by-step instructions. This book is designed to demystify the installation and setup of a home Linux server, making the process straightforward and accessible for anyone, regardless of their technical background.

By following this guide, you'll gain the knowledge and confidence to repurpose your existing hardware into a versatile server that meets your needs, whether for personal projects, learning, or small-scale server applications.

APPENDICES

Glossary of Terms

Apache2: A popular open-source web server software that serves web pages to users over the internet.

Backup: A copy of data or system files that is stored separately to ensure recovery in case of data loss or corruption.

CUPS (Common Unix Printing System): A modular printing system for Unix-like operating systems that allows a computer to act as a print server.

DNS (Domain Name System): A system that translates human-readable domain names (e.g., www.example.com) into IP addresses used by computers to locate each other on the network.

FTP (File Transfer Protocol): A standard network protocol used to transfer files between a client and a server over a network.

Firewall: A network security system that monitors and controls incoming and outgoing network traffic based on predetermined security rules.

Hostname: A label assigned to a device on a network that identifies it uniquely. It is used in URLs to identify a particular web page.

IP Address: A unique numerical address assigned to each device connected to a network that uses the Internet Protocol for communication.

MySQL: An open-source relational database management system that uses SQL (Structured Query Language) for accessing and managing databases.

Port Forwarding: A network configuration that redirects communication requests from one IP address and port number to another.

Postfix: An open-source mail transfer agent (MTA) used for routing and delivering email on Unix-like operating systems.

RAID (Redundant Array of Independent Disks): A data storage virtualization technology that combines multiple physical disk drive components into one or more logical units to improve performance and redundancy.

Static IP Address: A fixed IP address that does not change and is manually assigned to a device on a network.

Ubuntu: A popular open-source Linux distribution based on Debian, known for its user-friendly interface and ease of use.

User Permissions: The access rights assigned to user accounts and groups that determine what actions they can perform on files and directories.

VM (Virtual Machine): A software-based emulation of a physical computer that runs an operating system and applications as if it were a physical machine.

Web Server: A software application or hardware device that serves web pages to users over the internet.

Wildcard DNS Record: A DNS record that matches requests for any subdomain that has not been explicitly defined in DNS records.

Resources for Further Learning and Exploration

Continuous learning and exploration are essential for staying current with the latest advancements in home server technology.

Here are some valuable resources for further learning and exploration:

Online Courses and Tutorials:

Coursera: Offers courses on server administration, cloud computing, and containerization from top universities and organizations.

Udemy: Provides a wide range of courses on home server setups, Linux administration, Docker, Kubernetes, and more.

Pluralsight: Offers expert-led courses on virtualization, networking, and server management.

Online Communities and Forums:

Reddit: Subreddits like r/homelab, r/linuxadmin, and r/sysadmin are great places to ask questions, share experiences, and learn from the community.

Stack Overflow: A valuable resource for troubleshooting issues and finding solutions to specific technical problems.

GitHub: Explore open-source projects, contribute to code repositories, and collaborate with other developers.

www.ingramcontent.com/pod-product-compliance
Lightning Source LLC
Chambersburg PA
CBHW050104230526
45470CB00004B/1673